T0208642

ESSENCES OF TONGCHENG

MAUREEN ARMSTRONG

authorHOUSE®

AuthorHouse™
1663 Liberty Drive
Bloomington, IN 47403
www.authorhouse.com
Phone: 833-262-8899

Published by AuthorHouse 12/21/2023

ISBN: 978-1-6655-6295-9 (sc)
ISBN: 978-1-6655-6297-3 (hc)
ISBN: 978-1-6655-6296-6 (e)

Library of Congress Control Number: 2022911486

Print information available on the last page.

Credits to Tongcheng Teachers College.

Photographs by Maggie Ni.

This book is printed on acid-free paper.

Also by Maureen Armstrong

HORIZONS IN TONGCHENG
JULY'S DREAM BOOK 1

Acknowledgements

Special thanks to Hong Wei Wu for recommending this project, and for sharing our friendship with the English Department.

Thanks to Maggie Ni and meeting with President Shen of Tongcheng Teachers College to approve each of nineteen photographs to tell our reliable stories.

Most of all thanks to students for their interest, support, encouragement and precious time in their daily work to continue relationship building.

Contents

Introduction

Leafing through and reflecting upon pitiful but poignant images in family photographs and our comforting times together and now apart after 2010, write about challenges day after day. Years back after relocating and meeting new friends and neighbours learn one neighbour is writing serial romance novels in her home office. At one of our neighbourhood parties to share in celebrations writer mentions her choice to start each day is reading self-affirmation, writing in her journal and is loving watching each week television's new Seinfield show.

Yet journaling is as keeping childhood five-year diaries. Standing outside grandma's long-term care home in summer 2013, ponder how to describe to her writing our free-verse poetry journal. Experiences to share are from inspirations with mother, who believes in her daughter's skills in arts like watercolour painting and writing a book. Attending piano recitals, watching figure skating solo performances or level tests and writing our letters are common pleasures.

In 2009, soon at in-service training as volunteer tutor at a local college, learn English as a second language is like adjusting to acquiring physical or mental disability, speak below student abilities with one-two-syllables in words and meet with student for forty-five minutes twice each week. In *Essences of Tongcheng,* readers meet characters and visit places as if to learn when English is a second or foreign language.

In truth looking back into mediation work experiences before teaching English as a Foreign Language find an example, "I can speak three languages," client said.

"Does the client intend to represent the men's homeless shelter address written into log book as a permanent address?" colleague said.

Though friendships are trifles in lifestyles in Tongcheng. One perfect apple fits into one thin cardboard colourful gift box at Christmas wishing good thoughts and serenity students explain. Chronicles of gumption begin with your grandmother and me, and then alone in Tongcheng for free-verse poetry and art simulations, *Horizons In Tongcheng.*

Table of Photographic Contents

Series of nineteen photographs are inserted into pages with descriptions.

1. Book Cover

Tongcheng teachers college library is in the background with rust tiles; apartment is to very right on the second floor.

2. Part One Glimpses of Robust Times

The group photo is taken by President Shen at Celebration Farewell Dinner in June 2018.

Left to Right are Dean of English, David Wang, Dean of Physics, Headmaster Wu, myself, Maggie Ni, English Department colleague, Crystal, student assistant, Stephanie, student assistant

3. Part One Glimpses of Robust Times

Photo is taken by President Shen at Celebration Farewell Dinner June 2018.

Headmaster Wu is shaking Maureen's hand at the farewell celebration dinner.

4. Part Two Students From Tongcheng Teachers College (1904) Working With Maggie

One photo hiking with Maggie is of walking to viewpoint of the nearby Tongcheng Buddhist Temple in autumn 2016.

5. Part Two Students From Tongcheng Teachers College (1904) Working With Maggie

Two photos are at Jingzhu Temple Reservoir we visit 16 April 2017

6. Part Two Students From Tongcheng Teachers College (1904) Student Activities in English As Foreign Language Outside Foreign Teacher's Classroom

Five photos are of attending student-led holiday event in the lecture hall at Halloween English Corner fun event October 2016.

Photo 1) Standing in the middle masked students are on either side;

Photos 2)3)4)5) are of accepting package of tofu as sit amongst students in a lecture theatre.

7. Part Six Departing Tongcheng

One photo is of the Long Mian River flowing near Tongcheng.

8. Part Six Departing Tongcheng

Three photos are the new location for Tongcheng Teachers College campus sports track, close-up of building and distant view of college.

9. Part Six Departing Tongcheng

Three photos are of Guniubei Reservoir near Tongcheng city.

Author's Foreword

While reading the book, a lot of memories flooded my mind; the first time we met and all the good places we have traveled to. I was surprised of Maureen's ability to capture all the memories that took place in Tongcheng.

In Tongcheng Teachers' College, she was an excellent teacher and her teaching style impressed me a lot. She was more than a foreign teacher, we learned a lot from her with her proficiency in writing and her willingness to try new things and be accommodating of differences of all the people she came across.

To be included in the book and also be asked to write a blurb has been such an honor, especially seeing that she created a vivid picture of our city and college. This book for me, is a representation of how friendships can grow between people of totally different backgrounds and cultures. We are so grateful that our city gave her such memorable experiences and this serves as a reference book about Tongcheng culture, the people and the traditional Chinese culture.

In Chinese we say "杰作" (a master piece).
Maggi Ni

Preface

Free verse of becoming new Republic of Ireland citizen with passport is written while on vacation in Saskatchewan at summer seasonal home, an authentic homestead of immigrants.

IN MY FIRST LAND

There rests the rustic rural cottage,
a relic from past;
Shall we go for a walk,
To the rock bundle of meditation rock;
A place to ease struggling sorrows
Rising up for morrows;
Extinguishing the lust for all tomorrows. Maulo

Writing at nine o'clock in morning during walk around back ten acres, stop to sit at rock pile on homestead's land, and write with promise and to publish on mind for students of Tongcheng 11th of August 2021.

* * *

Maggie advises soon after arrival in September 2016, and after moving into apartment in Tongcheng, "Drink green tea to help for clear teaching voice."

Every day before class in Tongcheng from outset in September 2016, baby-blue electric kettle is plugged in first-thing after waking to make green leaf tea, and sits on floor of apartment in our first contract to teach English as a foreign language. In our second contract after returning to

Tongcheng College in October 2017, same baby-blue kettle from apartment last year with dishes and cooking pots is moved by students in September 2017, to sit on counter in small kitchen of second and new location of apartment on campus of Tongcheng Teachers College, and continue to make green leaf tea.

With backgrounds or descriptions to stories of times in Tongcheng from September 2016, our work together to improve abilities in speaking, listening, reading and writing English is written into words spread onto pages like magical veins but callous reminders.

Overseas teaching English as foreign language qualifications evolve with university degree from 1980. With many courses over five years to upgrade, achieve certificate in family mediation in 2008, took quick-step into good job in 2009, and beginnings of volunteer tutoring English as second language in 2009. Upon completing online course in spring 2015, with books to learn to teach English as foreign or second language, few months later in February 2016, answer orange ad in upper left corner of English as Foreign language employment internet page recruiting foreign teachers to China one quiet Saturday afternoon. Phone call offer 13th of March 2016, to work in China is beginning process to relocate.

In discussions with oldest son, Mark, in 2003, said, "Work to become foreign teacher is comparable to service industry employment, and can upgrade in courses online from same university attending for degree."

Mark said, "What of concerns for three younger brothers finishing high school?"

Without doubts with offer of contract in 2016, employment in China teaching English as foreign language overseas Mark said, "Isn't China a Communist country? Reminbi is their currency. I never thought of working in China."

Twenty-four hours pass to confirm contract with Chinese employer's email to complete employment contract with official government seal. Some duties employer requests are to apply for Z Visa at internet link, include two employment references and request criminal record check from local police authority. Part-time casual students' support employment and volunteer English as second language tutoring match for two employer references to apply for Z Visa to government of China.

Nor Tongcheng daily unique experiences are choices to mingle with old experiences. Now grandchildren and marriages or careers are evolving with three younger brothers. Reactions are congratulatory to be helpful leaving country to expect new, different, engaging results. Children applaud mother examining simple independence's abroad, overseas in China.

Since 2010, during and after daily walking for recovery from complex physical workplace injuries begin to illustrate or sketch and write in free verse form with pen name Maulo. To one journal first written with mother in 2013, two years of working and living in Tongcheng from 2016 to 2018, are written into two more journals as passions of various and multiple successes with good chances to meet new people different in politics, religions, physical colour, or work, and to write of daily life in Tongcheng, Province of Anhui.

Beginnings

Beginnings, in daily walks after 2012, are of picking-up pencils and carrying reusable envelopes to sketch, in reusing gifts of journaling books to write, of finding wax crayons and oil pastels at sales or around home and searching for reusable paper and simple uses of street-finds becoming perpetual daily activities to draw or write three dimensions of images familiar or new. Days pass until 2013, to take chance to defy separation to write together to record past passions hidden with delights to discover perfections. Our record together is written into seven free-four-line verses. Thoughts find hopes in newness, risk and search for discovery for any crack of time left in place to write again.

In truth after writing first journal with Mom, two journals follow in Tongcheng, Anhui, China. Walking eight kilometres to Mom's care home every second week begins one Saturday morning in July 2013, continuing until care home's Christmas celebrations. On first try couple hours to walk lengthy distance revisit public beach another two kilometres farther on past care home. Location is enjoyable in support of past times with Mom taking grandchildren to beach in hot summers, and to regain self-confidences. Today, and beginning ten kilometres walk back home in early afternoon, stop in at care home. After walking through front door ask permission from care aide, and gain entry into locked-ward to visit Mom.

In large community room Mom sits on bench of walking-aide with other patients nearby, "Hello Mom."

Mom speaking-up said, "We do not need you."

Without delay turning around leave care home. Walking early autumn week-end morning two weeks later, sign guestbook at front desk of same care home, and request opening locked door. Mom in mid morning wrapping warm in blanket, sits in wheelchair. with care aide standing nearby in same community room finding Mom two weeks earlier.

I said, "Is visiting two weeks earlier too stressful?"

Standing to her right and behind Mom, the care aide shaking her head said, "Condition is aging issue. Visit is fine."

Mom is staring and we smile to begin our first visit since 2010. During visits in autumn 2013, into hardcover journal book carrying in backpack for writing during daily walking, unwrap from cloth peach-orange flowery book cover and together begin to write. Either we sit together in large community room with Mom either propping up in bed or sitting upright in wheelchair in sunny kitchen.

Sitting together beside Mom sitting upright in mobile hospital bed, large window shows small green lawn with concrete path.

I said, "Do you walk on this path?"

Mom glances at path and she nods.

One occasion visit Mom in her private room. Standing at end of Mom's bed female care aide is tending to dressing changes.

Care aide said, "Fine to stay. Please stay close by."

Mom seems to be in pain and hold small sugar packet in hand empty from attending community coffee house. In Mom's view, as she lays in bed and care aide around her, with pencil draw sketch into small reusable paper with Mom's eyes in line of eye sight.

"Try to imagine a walk with me through this pain," I said,

Mom stares at me as stand at foot of her bed with care-aide tending, seeming to hear as closing her eyes as if to meditate or be peaceful as drawing sketch.

Two years pass before departure to Tongcheng August 2016. While retrieving passport and official Z Visa at Chinese Passport office, Patrick, a son, and Emily arrange Bed and Breakfast for four days and short walk from their small one bedroom apartment few weeks after first grandchild, Ada, is born in July 2016. Justin, a son, and girlfriend, Stacey, soon his wife, join us in apartment to order takeout Indian Asian dishes for lunch together to celebrate.

Most important in March 2017, in first foreign teaching contract of ten months in Tongcheng, while laying in bed relaxing at night after teaching English as foreign language classes discover homestead ten acres for sale online while researching property. Ten acres of original homestead land is dark and curious as look at photographs for hours deciding on progressing with offer to purchase. Location sits within one hour drive or fifty miles of Northern Irish immigrant grandparents' homestead from early 1920's. Owning property in area is lifestyle alternative to return to on summer vacations, and after departing Tongcheng, or to restore homestead shop into work-live-loft. After accepted purchase offer from China in spring of May 2017, complete sale in summer vacation away from Tongcheng Teachers College, and before returning to China in October 2017, and Tongcheng Teachers College.

Indeed during August sleep in family tent next to caragana hedge at homestead and begin shovelling and sweeping garage and attached workshop, and carrying and storing remnants of tools from abandonment to homestead's barn. Northern Irish grandparents build small cabin in 1950's, for short summer vacations in location one hour north at beach-lake resort.

Neighbour, who owns a cabin nearby, often stops to chat while passing by during holidays in mid 1980's, and said, "Only place he new of similar to resort is what he has read about China because of unique temperatures and trees that grow and resemble groves of poplars or elms lining natural sandy beach."

Conversations fill fantasies of history and life in China reading in novels as young girl.

In teen-age years father, who works in agriculture, said, "President Richard Nixon is visiting China, and first American President to visit Communist nation."

Years later in September 2016, new experiences are in remote area of Tongcheng, Province of Anhui in subtropical China. Spoken dialect of Tongcheng is unique and harsh to understand for students of college or others visiting from regions in Anhui or provinces in China, and where relocation is to work as English as foreign language teacher for two years. Qualities of guileful actions leading to betrayals from past are left for interests in present life-style in Tongcheng. Betrayal is theme in both free verse journals writing while living in Tongcheng, and in many free verses behaviours of betrayal are more or less valuable to resistance. Two journals describe essential parts of experiences from living on college campus.

On the contrary six years earlier after January 2010, before arriving in Tongcheng in 2016, next five years are daily events to adjust to being out-of-work with insurer's medical prognosis of no return to work. Training for motivation to good health comes from learning and leading past community volunteer groups in recoveries to healthy living experiences. Walking and running five to ten kilometres in daily schedule create personal strengths and endurance.

During period from January 2012, develop internet tag #filthydirtybuttonart and with son's, Justin's, recommendation apply for online account. Picking-up every piece of garbage in daily five to ten kilometre walking exercise, including picking-up empty beverage containers to carry and return for cash to Return-It-Depot, is sole income after job loss and injury. Cash fund from returning empties for refund accumulates to be enough to open new savings account, and use offer of bank credit card for line of credit to borrow and finance home. New savings account fund is accumulation of cash from returning empty beverage containers, and will become essential cash of six hundred dollars to travel to China. Garbage collected becomes useful in an imaginative manner too for reusing in new form.

Yet during walking from leaving and returning to permanent home, new activities from sketching, writing free verses, and photography are often on short stops to sit, and put into new online account, *Houseoftheredmug.* T-shirt designing becomes important part of developing internet tags *#filthydirtybuttonart* with colourful illustrations of fantasy original characters, Lily, Turshel and Fox inventing from backgrounds with parents or alone in childhood. Out of all day physical exercise and sketching, writing, drawing or photography, any experience is thought-out encouragement, and to begin to believe in use of abstract conversations to learn to speak, write, listen and read English in work career as creative foreign English teacher in conversational English as foreign language. While packing-up and leaving Tongcheng at end of two successive contracts teaching English as a foreign language write in journal notes.

June 25, 2018 4 days until departure

The heat is 90 degrees F. With 85% humidity
With no air conditioning in my apartment
I've washed some clothes
And will begin to plan to pack my bags
All my requests for assistance are complete
Continuing to walk 5 km before 10 am
Helps to ease a stomach cramp
Eating a meal is more difficult
Which I take some time to finish
There are strong warm winds.
From the south like tropical warm winds
I've seen pairs of lime green average-size birds
Flock on the ground and in the grape tree
The large grape tree is producing small green like lime balls
The size of large marbles falling to the ground
A lime green bird seems to peck at them is motioned
By a second lime green bird from a branch
They sit or perch facing the same direction
Then fly south away from the grape tree
The beige bandit birds of similar size
Do not appear today at the playground track. Maulo 16:17 hours Monday

PART ONE

GLIMPSES OF ROBUST TIMES

Tongcheng College Group Farewell LtR David, Dean of Physics, Headmaster Wu, Maureen, Maggie, Crystal, Stephanie

Undoubtedly, three free verse journals are progressive and related in thoughts from 2013, and Seven *Free Verse from China Journal (2016) With PuzzleOurTurtle (2013)* Journal. Second *Journal of Poetry from Tongcheng, Anhui (2017)* after arriving to teach English as Foreign Language. Into large notebook with notes to add to notes from tutoring write free verses or paragraphs as discussions of distances with past times riddled by betrayals, injuries and lost fortunes. Resting in evening January 2017, halfway through first ten-month contract teaching in Tongcheng, hoping to connect with old friends to invite to visit China, search addresses to find friend's loss of life in obituary posting online. Oldest son Mark agrees to request in email and notifies younger brother, Stuart, agreeable to posting family condolences. October 2017, third Journal From Tongcheng begins after returning with second ten-month contract teaching English as Foreign Language in Tongcheng speaking or writing to old friend of daily experiences, and write journal each late night before putting out lights for sleep.

More specifically moving overseas is relocation for employment rather than relocation as in homesteading like Irish grandparents although both adjustments prosper with sharing languages, multiple backgrounds, personal experiences and life skills. What compels people to learn new second or foreign languages? Beliefs in practicing conversations with abstract illustrations of any common experience are effective qualities in classroom and small group exercises in English as Foreign Language conversations. Therefore, students learn to use words from teaching and introducing groups of English words in weekly classroom lessons. Conversations are in small groups to practice describing varieties of activities to improve beginner to intermediate English speaking, listening, writing and reading skills.

Though Tongcheng Teachers College is in more southern subtropical Anhui Province close to cities Anqing and Hefei, choose Tongcheng with employer in Hangzhou for first foreign teaching ten-month contract. Social times for like hiking and meals or treats are with Maggie, college colleague and friend. When return to Tongcheng Teachers College in October 2017, new college textbook with sample exercises implements classroom led-conversations. Formal invitations are from student assistants, Crystal and Stephanie, to college activities but in more independent lifestyle in Tongcheng buy meals from street vendors on local streets, visit Bank of China for account pay cheque information, or shop at supermarket and markets for food and cooking as if familiar to living in Tongcheng one year later.

Undoubtedly, at faculty supper in nearby restaurant few weeks after first arriving in Tongcheng September 2016, David, Dean of English Department said, "What are first impressions of our students?"

Faculty sitting at round table listen to our discussion.

I said, "I am finding students very enjoyable and am grateful to students for respectfulness, participation and attentiveness in English as Foreign Language classroom."

Evolving to adore abilities in Tongcheng to visit temples, hear noisy streets, dwell in two traditional apartments, witness ancient street wagons with male or female pulling, walk through palm tree groves, and visiting local shops with helpful Tongcheng shopkeepers is beginning after arrival in early September 2016. Few days before classes are to begin colleagues are welcoming and friendly on campus often saying, "Hello" or "Hello Maureen" with name as if already meeting.

Since before arriving in Tongcheng in 2016, tutoring two adult South Korean female visitors locally in 2009, and 2013, are past historical events that are seeming like natural progressions to tutoring Tongcheng students in after-class time hours at college's playground location. Encouraging speaking, reading, writing and listening qualities are genial opportunities to speak English as a foreign language on any topic from music to boys, and through daily sharing college issues.

In last month working in Tongcheng June 2018, freshman student speaking-up in class said, "Will you write about us after leaving Tongcheng?"

"Since writing is enjoyable will try," I said to smiling female student.

Classmates join her smile with more students' smiles.

Yet selections of topics tell about teaching college classes with students, two new apartment homes, new friends, and visiting family either together or by internet and virtual online visits while living in Tongcheng in Anhui Province of southeast subtropics of vast China. Hong Wei Wu, wife of Headmaster Wu of Tongcheng College, writing after leaving Tongcheng is sending love she is feeling every day from meeting three times in back-to-back two ten-month contracts in Tongcheng. Hong becomes new and renewing friendship after departing Tongcheng. From official college end-of-term supper in late December 2017, our introduction is mixed into holiday gift arrangement from her husband, Headmaster Wu, and is scheduled in city of Anqing. Maggie, college adviser is asked to accompany trip in college car in next few days.

Headmaster Wu sitting to right, and Maggie on left said, "You are to enjoy ice cream."

In May 2017, Hong Wei Wu meets second time after meeting in Anqing December 2016, when Hong comes with Maggie to college to meet at apartment with many traditional gifts to celebrate Dragon Boat Festival. Hong brings famous zongzi sticky rice wrapped in bamboo and packages of Muslim traditional tasty maple-syrup squares made in Anqing. Several cooked duck eggs are given away to Maggie to share to colleagues. We walk together down Long Mian Avenue with Hong carrying her umbrella to stay out of sun wondering if heat is too much, window shop a bit and tell both women of granddaughter as pass children's clothing. Nearby large tea-house is open and we order soft drinks and food together.

Hong, sitting beside in bench seat on-right, is adjusting shoulder wrap she wears, and with Maggie translating said, "Shoulder is painful from bursitis."

"I wear yellow-brimmed hat with country's flag pin, carry backpack instead of using umbrella, and strengthen back and shoulders. Carrying umbrella and purse causes pain too," I said turning to Hong.

Hong is listening and said in English, "Maybe try backpack and hat but maybe looks bad."

After our drinks, and snack we leave tea house together, and bid Hong good-bye outside. Maggie said, "Hong will join teaching colleagues from Anqing she travels with by bus and are attending meetings in Tongcheng."

After departing Tongcheng in June 2017, and return-trip to Tongcheng in October 2017, Hong's third and final meeting arrangements are in Hong's text 07 April 2018, telling of visit to Tongcheng in afternoon to her mother's Tongcheng home, asking to arrange casual meeting. Hong arrives with *Qingming* Festival food gifts for festival, in English words is Tomb Sweeping Day, to honour past loved ones. Outside in front of apartment building on street and in view of college front gate Hong's husband, Headmaster Wu, is standing aside as meeting Hong.

Headmaster Wu shaking Maureen's hand at farewell celebration June 2018

Leaving apartment building and walking towards college gate, Headmaster Wu is in background. Hong speaking first said, "Maria, my friend."

We hug.

"Glad to meet too," I said.

We speak a bit about departing.

Hong said, "There is my husband there."

Hong in times is mentioning husband is working most days and to find something to do fills time to write and publish children's poetry books. Another college member brings bags from black sedan and Hong is sharing large variety of specialty items for *Qingming* Festival.

Hong writing 12 July 2018, after final departure said, "Have your sons seen you? Your Chinese experience must be a legend."

Hong writing soon again about researching historical Tongcheng and academic influences and sending photographs said, "I went to Tongcheng last week. It was taken in the Old Street of KongCheng."

Most important after returning to Tongcheng for second contract in October 2017, Thursday night is favourite night at Tongcheng College with night classes once-a-week for Flight Attendant Certificate students. These enthusiastic students are added to schedule in October 2017, filling in eighteen classes each week of schedule requirements for faculty. Before class begins original lessons are written on simple greetings, for example speaking with passengers or personal introductions.

First-time entering classroom about forty-five students are in class. Students cooperate with taking attendance on blank sheet of paper with writing names, and later initials for attendance dates or student check marks noting attendances as weeks progress. Lessons on one vocabulary word and passenger management, such as flight attendant's self introduction and offering services, are in two forty-five minute classes with short ten minute break in between. To begin class start English vocabulary and speaking exercise from writing with chalk on green chalkboard class's English as a Foreign Language lesson date and one English vocabulary word next to Chinese teacher's lesson and writing in Chinese from earlier in day.

After two weeks of classes female student, sitting in front on left in rows of wooden, blue desks and classroom monitor, runs next door for copy of Flight Attendant Certificate textbook. Textbook is written in scripts of activities for flight attendants. We begin to read and speak together English conversations from textbook as whole class and in small groups. Students' request tutoring from textbook for next day's English speaking skills test with Chinese teacher. Later in next class students share success stories with Chinese teacher's description of improvement from results of practice in English as Foreign Language classes for their Chinese teacher's business English class. Students range from skilled intermediate to students with beginner skills to speak English in small groups. Circling around classroom for half-hour of forty-five minutes is developing confident students who may even speak-up in greeting in English at mealtimes in canteen.

Student assistant, Stephanie, is coming to apartment after six pm in evening to walk together to Flight Attendant Certificate students' classroom. Across college street from apartment and in window view with front gardens to college buildings, two academic buildings with six stories are in right-angle shapes with stairs between floors like zigzags. Up marble staircase we walk two flights to classroom for forty to fifty students. At nine pm in evening Stephanie is returning to hallway outside classroom windows to stand waiting or outside open classroom's door to walk together down staircase and out building.

Marble staircase landing is with wide entrance-way and glass doors leading outdoors of building onto wide concrete and marble platform with shallow stairs to sidewalk on left. One warm dark evening, fierce spring subtropical rainstorm with lightening streaming across sky, and colliding with black Tongcheng high-rise buildings and skyline, is blowing rain into doorways to waiting students mostly running to dormitories. Stephanie is always thoughtful and brings umbrella.

Palm trees are silhouetted in green space to left between college's buildings and border dark green mountain in twilight. The walkway is tiled and street lights are lighted for our walk together short distance past library on our left to cross street to apartment building with residents' apartment lights shining in darkness in six-storey apartment building. To right we pass mature thirty-foot tall palm trees growing on front lawn of college buildings circling gold-spoke globe sculpture posing on ceramic tiles and projecting into darkness thirty-feet high. Stephanie walks on either side in these walks. College's large library building lights are on and open in evenings until ten pm in evening. Magnolia trees on left crossing street are twenty-feet tall lining street we must cross to apartment building. Many faculty and staff members live with families and is new location for foreign teacher's apartment in building with comfortable three bedroom large apartments, kitchens and modern three piece bathrooms. Walking at night is an activity managing with invitations and student assistants to official events. Relaxation after classes in this walk is intensifying with experiences of palm trees in night under lights and magnolia tress with white spring blossoms the size of volleyballs oozing with sweet aromas out of hot-pink centres.

Speaking to Stephanie one evening, during our spring walk later in March 2018, couple weeks after Term Two begins said, "It smells like rain."

Stephanie laughing in her buoyant bubbling reply said, "I adore impressions in speaking English."

After leaving Tongcheng in June 2018, in text to Stephanie said, "Favourite times in Tongcheng are of later in day in our walks from Flight Attendants classes in darkening twilight and near magnolia trees with large, shiny, green, umbrella leaves and sweet spring aromas.

Stephanie messaging said, "The walks were the sweetest moments."

One night after walking back to apartment in darkness and after Flight Attendants class in spring March 2018, make decision to reply in texting to Eva to refuse third contract to teach English as Foreign Language in China. Later in sunny morning in June 2018, with Maggie walk to building of classrooms where English as Foreign Language classrooms for two years are located on second floor.

In distance as man is walking towards us Maggie said, "Handsome man is human resource staff member responsible for foreign teacher."

We all smile at each other with greetings.

Moreover Maggie, new colleague, and with Dean David, supervisor of English department, tell after first arrival in Hefei two years earlier in September 2016, and meeting at fast train station, air is very clean in Tongcheng due to closeness of college next to mountain.

Maggie is walking together to college's oval sport track next to low green mountain after classes during first days in Tongcheng said, "Sport track is called playground."

Canteen is source of social times and location to once in awhile accept invitations to join meal with senior students or even tutor new students. Joanna, first student assistant for advice and help after arriving in 2016, joins for any meal like breakfast or supper during first term in canteen but refuses canteen food in second term choosing to eat in restaurants.

At supper early after arriving in 2016, Joanna said, "Squash porridge is good for supper and digestion unlike steamed rice giving stomach aches."

After returning to Tongcheng in October 2017, during second ten-month contract, often choose rice and vegetables and meat, and becoming more typical for supper-time meals, or boiled eggs and porridge or steamed buns and fried dumplings. Daily walking on college's playground, artificial sports field track surface, next to green mountain is where poplar trees grow and line northern corner of oval track. Poplar trees are smaller on edge of playground with slender trunks rising fifteen feet. Mountain is filled with trees resembling pine trees and in early springs white and later pink blossoms appear in mixed variety of forest trees. The rustling leaves of poplar trees on corner of playground in warm winds becomes an anchor as months and seasons change resembling sounds of thoughtful times.

Though Spring Festival celebration is in China, February 2019, mail packet of postcards and stickers for thank-you's and gifts for freshman students from last term's first year English Class in 2017 to 2018, is arriving at Tongcheng College's library and delivery by China Post. In continuation of our work together in speaking English as foreign language, Maggie opens internet online English Corner student group where Donna, Crystal, Tiffany, Joanna, Molly, Cathy and Joy and others may share discussions.

Maggie sends emoji and text message for information about the package and said, "Trick, trick, trick the cute sophomore students. Staff and students continue to miss their foreign teacher."

On the other hand at Tongcheng Teachers College music playing announcing times of classes starts at six in morning until nine in evening. Very close to end of terms in December or June music disappears, and feel or hear quiet with relief. In rarer occasions male or female speaking from loudspeakers like radio shows mostly in morning are heard occasionally walking to canteen and going for breakfast.

One time Maggie said, "Announcements are broadcasts."

Walking daily at playground in spring until end of June 2018, repeat to myself and said, "There will always be next year's freshman class."

PART TWO

STUDENTS FROM TONGCHENG TEACHERS COLLEGE (1904)

FIRST GREETINGS

View of Tongcheng from Buddhist Mountain hiking with Maggie 2016 to 2017

Jingzhu Temple Reservoir, visit site with Maggie spring 2017

Most important after arriving in Tongcheng in August 2016, two students are sent by the college to meet me in lobby at hotel the first morning at eight am. Annie and Sherlock, freshman students, are friendly as we start to walk down the street called Longmian West Road. Annie later becomes my first student to tutor at the college's playground beginning the following March in seven months.

Our first stop my first morning in Tongcheng is at the food fair across and down the street with fast food stands and people cooking at each stand. A pancake is purchased for me by Annie but resembles a wrap with eggs and some meat.

"Thank you Annie," I said in English and then begin to enjoy the pancake standing in the sunshine. Twenty vendors or more are amidst the cooking and preparing of a variety of noodles and rice dishes, drinks and fruit. Next spring becoming fond of the pineapple on a stick sold by the vendor at the front gate return to food fair.

With Annie and Sherlock leave food fair, turn left to pass street entrance to Buddhist temple painted in a mustard yellow where we step inside the door.

Sherlock after going inside the temple and returns said, "We must leave as services resume."

We continue across the street and turn right at the corner to walk past businesses to the end of a street where the Bank of China bank is located. Days before after arriving in China and stopping in Hangzhou, foreign teacher tells me the Bank of China is the sign for bank on corner is bank to use for international bank transfers. Across the street from bank the Bank of China, the local landmark and national historic Confucian temple is closed. Photographs of myself in front of the temple are taken by Sherlock who emails them to me to send to my family.

In the area students said, "Six Foot Alley Name is walking lane we try and very beautiful."

Annie is quiet and kind with an affectionate personality and at least five foot seven with a high English speaking high beginner to intermediate English speaking level skill. Sherlock is a warm and carefree young adult, solidly built, about five foot five, wears glasses and speaks beginner English. Sherlock shares later in class of future travel to the United States to visit her sister, a foreign student.

Sherlock loves colours and green ivy crawling over the top of the wall as she stands to touch the trailing ivy and turning said, "Very beautiful. Beauty is in green colour."

This Six Foot Alley is six feet wide and is used by local people to walk inside the city block and away from the street. Annie stands nearby.

As we leave the Six Foot Alley, we walk short distance to supermarket located in large building with front thick plastic panels, a doorway we walk through. At back of this room, Annie and Sherlock teach how to check backpacks in lower floor lockers fitted with tickets and an electronic lock. Tickets open lockers after shopping. Small shops on entrance level sell children's clothing, personal hair items and other clothing.

We take the escalators to second floor and up to third floor where we walk around large and said, "I want to buy some bananas."

Bananas are put into bag by students and walk to check-out. Next to cashier security guard asks students questions at check out. These questions, Annie and Sherlock explain are of their relationship to foreigner shopping.

We took a taxi back to college where we walk-around lower campus area and past an apartment building to stop and enjoy seeing potted peppers ripening in short-tiled-walkway and in front of the apartment building I will live in next year. Two students discuss tour of campus and Annie suggests we visit canteen to be able to choose meals.

We turn around to walk two blocks past student residences to canteen. Canteen office sits to right on main floor of large two-storey canteen building and is fitted with sliding glass windows. We are welcomed into the canteen's office by staff, and only time ever am inside this office, as we are seated with canteen clerk. Annie asks me about Renminbi cash I carry to pay canteen staff fifty yuan for credit on new canteen card clerk provides. Female staff canteen clerk with auburn hair advising to add fifty yuan to canteen's lunch card she is giving to me and to come every week to buy credit on card. Often seeing this clerk, clerk is driving her electric car to canteen and parks in front.

On walking back to hotel Sherlock and Annie together said, "What do you miss?"

"Coffee," I said.

Soon one day Sherlock and Annie bring Nescafe small packets of coffee they purchase from supermarket as gift in class.

"Amazing, thank you," I said.

Coffee packets are divided in half for use twice for watery coffee blends.

WORKING WITH MAGGIE, TONGCHENG TEACHERS COLLEGE ADVISER

On the mountain of Buddhist's temple, from college to base of mountain nearby Tongcheng and passenger on Maggie's pink e-bike, we hike Sundays up main mountain road. After returning to Tongcheng one Sunday afternoon, Maggie asking to share lunch, and at nearby restaurant to college said, "Please share your writing?"

"Try to find title, *Two Spruce* as entry into website hobby like in my resume submitting before departure to China. Four lines of free verses in one and two syllable words are in an English as Foreign Language folder to locate the free verse."

Maggie holds her phone to search for poetry hobby.

The content of English as foreign language classroom is assisted with feedback from students to Maggie, an instructor from college's English department. Maggie is given task of being foreign teacher's adviser as both of us are female so our relationship develops. For example, in first of two consecutive ten-month contracts, Western holidays like Christmas or Thanksgiving are topics students request in student evaluations for lesson planning. After returning, ignoring these holidays in lessons is Maggie's advice from students sharing information on feedback to interests in learning conversational English.

Free time includes students at sport track called the playground for daily walk.

To Maggie said, "Can tutoring invitations be for to anyone walking at playground to walk together at sport track with me to practice their English speaking and listening skills?"

Day later walking and tutoring at playground is approved by David, Dean of English and Maggie. In request for permission for walking at the playground, offer tutoring to any student who will walk with me. Maggie is sharing information with David, and agreement becomes tutoring activities. Tutoring for competitions is reviewing background information from paper study-booklet of tasks to tutor students for preparation in provincial competitions in neighbouring college at Hefei, capital city one hour by car. For ten weeks, during two springs of each contract in two years at Tongcheng Teachers College, walking at playground becomes tutoring location with students practising for competitions.

In September 2016, one woman brings music player to playground in late afternoon for evening's square dance local women attend but sometimes few female students try to dance as well. Students try to learn dancing from local women. Soon after arrival, in one of these darkening evenings after square dancing begins, walk down brick lane with Maggie after walking at playground together where the evening square dancing begins. To leave playground, Maggie pulls back closed-gate, and we walk down wide concrete staircase to brick lane and bamboo growing nearby. Experience is moving enough to return to this lane during daytime on weekend to interpret four large engravings in granite lining exterior wall of brick lane. High retaining wall for this lane is below apartment faculty residences and student residences and housing. Viewing and description of engravings is weekend task for free-time activity. Private tutoring notebook, packing into luggage departing in August 2016, contains eight months of tutoring notes. In fact same notebook in Tongcheng begins with free verses after arrival and notes of etchings on granite.

Free Verse China September 07, 2016

Walking Under The Moon
The track is very light
The 'best there is'
But to look up and see
The shimmering slice of a silver moon
Frustrated by clouds that distract;
The first quarter shines
After the cloud's pass
For a blue sky that is extending far. Maulo

September 16, 2016 *The Moment Was Waiting*
Uphill is not simple
But then the lines formed
A tall colour is shown
And I stand in awe at first
As my differences show myself. Maulo

September 17, 2016 *The Staircase from Playground*

First Bamboo

Square polished granite blocks describe four separate Wall Murals engraved and to the left many Chinese letters.

1. *Seems to describe doctor's office; Dr. sits at desk speaking to standing patient. Ornate desk; bookcase behind Dr. Chair; scroll to Dr.'s right on wall with floor covered in treasure boxes of books;*
2. *Student visits teacher who seems to instruct. Both are standing; desk behind teacher; many books and teaching tools;*
3. *Street scene with priest wearing hair in long braid administering to merchant and family. Two women attendants.*
4. *Priest visits country and farmer; wife carries rod on back with two baskets of rice. Farmer stands touching cone-shaped hat as priest stares away towards front with fan. We are his audience. Attendant stands with priest. Rice paddies are in background against mountain view.*

– Bamboo shoots stand between polished granite murals and the roof top above looks like cake icing edging. Maulo

In December 2016, one afternoon before end of first-term celebration dinner with Headmaster Wu, Maggie's suggestion is to go for walk to nearby community park. We walk together after meeting at college down lengthy Long Mian avenue to cross street to park.

During our walk to park Maggie said, "I grade students on their English as Foreign Language from your records of students' classroom attendance. If student attends all classes top grade ninety percent is given; if attendance is poor sixty percent."

After jay-walking crossing street to park, we walk together on asphalt wide path around to central area duck pond to stop to enjoy few ducks swimming and stand together on small man-made pond's deck in overcast late December afternoon with no visitors to park and some concrete-like statues near pond. Across pond is security guard house and washrooms. We continue to walk around park on asphalt path to gate and food stands, and Maggie buys us BBQ pork-on-a-stick.

We leave to walk left out of same park-gate to reach busy street, and turn right to walk down sidewalk past garages and northeastern side of Tongcheng's mountain when Maggie said, "Mountain is used for tombs in past but now burning is preferable due to available space on mountain."

We walk past businesses and busy garages to turn right to walk through concrete tunnel with sidewalk on either side and said, "Are there problems with graffiti painting inside tunnel?"

"Graffiti painting is serious issue and removal is same day," Maggie said.

Then walking through the tunnel leading us back to Longmian West Road, pass shops and restaurants to walk to restaurant on Longmian West Road.

I said, "How about taking this walk by myself?"

Maggie said, "Ask students to walk with you is good plan."

We arrive at restaurant for faculty celebration with headmaster.

More specifically three months later in March of 2017, nearing eighth month of first ten-month contract freshman student, Annie, asks me to join her to walk to same community park. Twice on one weekend we wander around same asphalt path, as with Maggie in December 2016. Spring visitors are flying kites and now park is with parents and children at busy playground built on bright blue cushions, rubber-like Annie explains, made from recycled tires and tutor Annie for upcoming annual provincial college level English speaking and comprehension competition.

In occasion of oldest son's and wife's visit in Tongcheng for Christmas in 2016, rain is pouring down in December and three of us stand on street outside supermarket after shopping.

Maggie drives by on her e-bike and is covered in her rain gear but stops and said, “Hello.”

“Hello Maggie. Please meet son, Mark and wife Jin visiting from Seoul, South Korea. Maggie is colleague and college adviser,” I said.

Mark and Jin together said, “Hello, hello.”

Sixteen to twenty-two year old students are assisted from our work together to learn to speak English fluently. After arriving in early September 2016, Headmaster Wu sends gift tin of tea, Headmaster purchasing in Shanghai, with Maggie to apartment to enjoy throughout next ten months. On this occasion Maggie’s mention of drinking green tea is especially helpful for clear teaching voice.

Hiking in November, Maggie suggests progressing up mountain to tea fields. Jumping at chance, we start and soon see vast tea fields with views of river. Tea will be harvested in March and huts are empty of tea field workers. During warm Sunday afternoon in spring of 2016, Maggie suggests going for ice cream. While we enjoy ice cream at busy and popular Western-food restaurant and Maggie’s treat, Maggie tells of local trend for meeting people on internet where married men seek out single girls.

“I am feeling bothered as own Mother calls too often and wants to show talk of concerns for staying single. I am told of married woman choosing to take chance with this older man she meets at work who is even married and has one child. Fifty percent of marriages is divorce rate in large cities in China. In smaller cities like Tongcheng, little divorce occurs. In large cities couples with young children often divorce breaking up young family,” said Maggie.

Most important in October 2017, after departing Tongcheng and returning to teach English as foreign language at Tongcheng Teachers College, previous year’s friendship with Maggie continues and follows us into this next consecutive ten-month contract. From apartment’s view of palm trees growing in circular pattern in front of college’s two main six-storey buildings in January 2018, first heavy snow fall covers and litters palm trees of second winter in Tongcheng. Maggie wonders if shoes are warm and safe enough but ask of playing in snow across street on lawn, and together make names in snow and together build very small snowman. Maggie takes photos of little snowman we make in snow and we sign our names in snow laughing and enjoying friendly snowball throwing. We walk past a group of male colleagues working in college's library Maggie waves to and all smile walking past palm trees covered in snow.

"Will palm trees grow again in spring?" I said.

"First snowfall is in twenty-five years covers these same pine trees. Trees are certain to survive," Maggie said.

"I think you mean palm trees," I said.

STUDENT ASSISTANTS JOANNA, CRYSTAL AND STEPHANIE

Student assistant, Joanna is assuming all helpful duties for foreign teacher in September 2016, in first teaching English as foreign language ten-month contract in Tongcheng. In second ten-month consecutive contract, Stephanie and Crystal assume all student assistant duties for keeping-up with information-sharing for their English as foreign language teacher, informing teacher of student English Corner activities, and help with day to day demands. English as foreign language teacher student assistant is requiring confident English speaking and listening skills to communicate with foreigner, and students serious about success in college studies capable of managing extra tasks. Student assistants are assessed by English department for student assistant volunteer. All three students are second year sophomore students.

Undoubtedly in first ten-month contract on January 07, 2017, Joanna walks together to supermarket to shop, and offers her cell phone number as a red card for savings discounts at check-out.

Joanna said, "I wonder of concern for knowing of skill to buy food in shops or supermarket. College canteen closes for two months, January and February between first and second terms."

Joanna tries to sign-up my own red card at supermarket's service desk but supermarket staff refuse. Day later Joanna helps send four envelopes to celebrate Chinese New Year to close family members from China Post, across the street from supermarket.

Joanna said, "Oh my goodness. Each envelope will be opened by China Post before arrival."

"I agree to opening envelopes," I said.

Joanna walks often together at playground, and easing adjustments to living in Tongcheng and on college campus helps in Mandarin pronunciation for two common introductions *Zaoshang hao* as good morning or *Xiawu hao* as good afternoon. When repairmen must come to apartment, Joanna arrives at request for help with translations, and assists to ship first gift package of tea overseas and is escort to student-led functions. Our photograph is taken in June 2017, with group of female students attending English Corner Joanna arranging.

After arrival in September 2016, to Joanna said "I cannot figure out use and struggle with ATM bank machines to withdraw cash?"

Joanna said, "Most banks offer English choice at ATM."

Joanna will accompany meeting at local bank to open bank account with letter from college for employment reference Maggie arranges and Joanna fills out form to obtain bank card to withdraw cash.

My son, Patrick, in texting said, "During travel see many disappointed travellers paying high rates to carry shopping or gifts onto plane airport staff will allow."

At college's shipping office day before departure from Tongcheng in June 2017, Joanna comes to apartment with two male classmates to help to arrange to ship recent gift boxes of green tea overseas from farewell meal evening before meal, and too much weight and size to carry onto plane.

Moreover after departing and returning to college in October 2017, during second ten-month contract sophomore student assistants Stephanie offers help at bank to complete bank transfers overseas, and both her and Crystal, are guides to student-led English Corner events. With sharing tasks Crystal and her college boyfriend, who also works at the college, install college's internet network connection in apartment when arrive in October 2017. Crystal and Stephanie help with extra information in first weeks for schedule of repairs to apartment's bathroom. With students' translations from college maintenance and repairman's schedules to install new tile in shower room, new flush toilet work is complete, and both assist with messages to and from Maggie.

Yet often while meeting Stephanie or Crystal will answer more requests and said to Stephanie, "Please interpret large gold ball sculpture being held up by thin rod with shiny spikes and sitting on flat tiled area in front lawns amidst palm trees perimeter, and doorways to two multi-storey adjoining academic buildings and palm trees.

Stephanie said, "Sculpture represents college holding up students to learn."

More specifically for two years Joanna, Stephanie or Crystal accompany for going or returning from all evening classes or events from apartments. During Joanna's student assistant's help in second ten-month contract students are available from September 2016 to June 2017, seldom are classes in evening's schedule except for Joanna helps to plan for son, Mark's, visit when college agrees to reschedule classes in evening so days off can be taken with visiting family. During Stephanie's and Crystal's student assistant schedules from October 2017 to June 2018, second ten-month contract schedule are available to accompany to walk from apartment to classes in foreign teacher's English as foreign language schedule, and attend regular evening classes.

TUTORING STUDENTS AT COLLEGE PLAYGROUND

Annie is first student to tutor in March 2017. On a Saturday morning while in my apartment and after two month winter holiday, David texts to meet Annie, a freshman student to tutor. Annie arrives at my apartment and we leave for a walk. Annie describes competition as becoming more important to her than college exam she is able take next year. After we meet in the morning for practice speaking English in a conversation, Annie provides thick pile of papers to review in preparation for these tutoring sessions to review later in apartment for our future tutoring sessions. We walk towards college's playground, and up brick lane past wall of granite engravings of traditional Chinese events. Annie speaks in English to me to interpret images.

As we are speaking together about the engravings and the stories, Annie translates into English from Chinese letters describing the engravings. Annie adding detail said, "1. the doctor is offered money; 2. the child's mother will make the teacher a coat as the teacher is very poor; 3. the local lord will solve the neighbourhood dispute; 4. taxes are paid by serfs on the rice field to tax collector."

David texts Annie to invite us to lunch. So at our lunch together Annie mentions her parents run a tea shop she must work in her parents' tea shop during her college holiday.

The following year March 2018, Stephanie, also foreign teacher student assistant, is sophomore student to tutor while walking at college's playground for same competition. Pages of handouts are brought by Stephanie as she says she is becoming more serious in her studies. On sunny spring day in same month, Maggie brings a student unknown to me and from faculty of teaching to playground to tutor and papers with descriptions written in English for tutoring. Three of us walk around playground track evaluating competition papers and discussing tutoring schedules. This student's English speaking skill seems similar to Stephanie's skill, and English Major students in English as Foreign Language classes.

On evenings of sub-finals for both years in college competitions attend competitions in classrooms and judge students on their pronunciation and comprehension. One evening in April 2017, is with also a visiting Chinese male teacher sitting beside my chair, and who visits with Dean David Wang. On this occasion David stands at end of competition to ask to Chinese teachers of lack of student competencies and mentions his gratitude to assistance as native English speaker.

One student on meeting to tutor at playground outside class said, "Stephanie is very beautiful."

Stephanie competes in provincial competition the next year in May 2018, in Hefei to achieve third place. When discussing the competition, Stephanie shares disappointment with third place finish.

"Parents are attending to watch her speak English but stand at back but leave room too soon," Stephanie said.

Students are aware of voluntary tutoring opportunities while walking at college's playground. Students from English as Foreign English classes or occasionally other faculties join individually or in pairs to walk together to practise speaking in conversational English about college experiences, personal interests and impressions of foreign culture. On walk up hill from canteen, or from English as Foreign Language classroom, any student or group of students might start conversations or to walk with me. In walk student mentions fantasy dream to experience climate of western country with feeling of outdoor cold and snow. In Tongcheng subtropical region, palm trees and bamboo grow well with humid hot weather in summer or winters without snow or extreme outdoor cold weather. Some may mention dreams to experience freedom, to travel overseas, or relationships with family or classmates, and are examples for classroom discussions to include students choosing countries they dream of visiting.

ENGLISH AS FOREIGN LANGUAGE CLASSROOM

Walking to classrooms from apartment or canteen arrive ten minutes early before scheduled class with English Major, Hotel Management, Japanese Majors, Flight Attendant Certificate or Tourism Certificate students.

"Do I arrive on time or early to class?" I said before very first classes in September 2016.

"Arrive ten minutes before classes begin," Maggie said.

Hotel Management classes in first contract are in another building, and run between classrooms from English Major foreign language classroom in three-storey smaller building to Hotel Management class in academic six-storey buildings. Dean Wang asks one student to demonstrate short-cut to pass through small garden on boulevard outside English Major classes near college front entrance to run between classes during morning schedule. Hotel Management students often are waiting.

Meanwhile arriving ten minutes early can welcome students. With few English words speak to students arriving to class and chatting often in hallway to classmates. Students and myself stand together until female college administration staff monitor arrives to open the classroom. Returning for second contract in October 2017, discover monitor is married to senior college administrator. They are neighbours in apartment on sixth floor of same apartment building, and are neighbours across the hall from David, Dean of English, and his family also on sixth floor. Only two apartments are on each floor of six-floor apartment building. In stairwell returning or departing apartments classroom monitor, meet neighbour and greet in Mandarin.

Near end of contract year in first spring term in June 2017, one manager and one workman arrive at English as foreign language classroom after class is over to start tearing apart desks, and so I said, "Where are classes going to be held?"

Maintenance manager said, "Renovations are to begin and ask Dean Wang for advice for where to complete the classes in term."

After texting Maggie discover classes next and final week of spring term will remain in same classroom as each class is kept until the end of term.

After returning to Tongcheng College, for our second contract, English as foreign language classroom is down long hallway from classroom year before now renovated to a computer laboratory classroom. Photographic portraits of Great Wall and Tienanmen Square are placed on both walls for length of hallway to glass windows of stairwell to fire escape to enjoy viewing while arriving ten minutes early to class and waiting for college monitor to arrive to open classroom door with the key. From glassed stairwell time permits to watch students coming and going to class on main avenue. In June near end of second contract close to final departure from Tongcheng in 2018, stand in stairwell to enjoy this poetic location of palm trees, flowering hedges and students coming and going sometimes like with a river of umbrellas either for heat or rain.

These classrooms are on second floor of the three-storey academic building. Walking into building on wide front entrance, in early morning for eight o'clock freshman classes, freshman student monitors assist arriving. Inside broad entrance hard granite floor leads to one wide staircase crammed with students in morning and later. One student with severe limp struggles and later enjoy seeing her striving to walk without limp at playground doing laps.

In 2016, classroom's view looks out onto college's entrance gate with cars coming and going and large circular welcome boulevard but through huge Chinese letters in shiny gold bronze on window's platform. With moving English as foreign language classroom across hallway short distance in October 2017, and returning to Tongcheng Teachers College for our second contract, view through large wall of windows looks out onto entrance to college's canteen. Both classrooms are filled with desks bolted to floor for fifty students learning to speak conversational English as a Foreign Language.

Our first classroom task each year is to fill in homemade paper name tags with English names chosen by students. These names are also copied into class rosters to maintain and create to record attendances. Each student writes chosen English names and adds initials to class roster on plain white bonded paper for attendances upon entering classroom. We all learn each others' English names in class. Bringing no paper in my packing to class must ask Maggie to help for white bond paper, and after returning for second year colleague in physical education in offices accepting request as turn up in office doorway giving more than enough,

"Ask for more paper if need," said tall and lean physical education teacher.

Often seeing teacher at playground, one time walking in heavy rain at playground year before and tormented at night by sounds of mice and static in wall, see what believe is dead mouse on track.

"Mouse," I said running up to teacher.

He nods and begins texting on cellphone.

Indeed during classes conversations begin often with students.

First term in Tongcheng October 2016, students said, "Maggie describes to them you complete dream to see Yangtze River?"

"Yes," I said. "Maggie accompanies their foreign teacher to complete Foreign Resident Permit in Anqing which sits next to the Yangtze River."

At term's end in December 2016, or December 2017, or June 2017, and June 2018, sophomores or freshman Molly and friends or students from either first or second year take photos in classrooms with their foreign teacher at end of classes.

Dean Wang visits in apartment in October 2017, day returning to Tongcheng said, "new textbook is provided by college and provides new lesson plans. Never correct students."

Students from English Major classes often give their foreign teacher Christmas gifts. A foil package of English Breakfast tea is gift from first year English Major student, who wraps her gift in a sports section of Western English newspaper in December 2017. The Western country's Sears company's Christmas catalogue brought in packaging that circulates in classes for fashion interests either year, but sits on teacher's desk dormant to lessons and available.

STUDENT ACTIVITIES IN ENGLISH AS FOREIGN LANGUAGE OUTSIDE FOREIGN TEACHER'S CLASSROOM

Throughout terms invitations from student assistants are to attend student official events.

Joanna said, "English Corners held in evening occur on Western holidays such as Halloween or Christmas. Possibly you attend?"

Foreign teacher's interest in students' activities is in extra time as college activity and in addition to fifteen hours of classes each week. At these events, many students from sophomore and freshman classes attend. Student leaders plan events for these English Corner groups, who meet together to share an understanding of Western culture.

Halloween English Corner student-led event 2016 to 2018

Invitations arrive in texts or in person from student assistants to English Corners. After returning to Tongcheng College, more of these events are held in large lecture-style classroom with theatre seating. Halloween is always popular. In second Christmas 2017, English Corner speak of family's tradition of baking sugar cookies from cutting shapes, baking and decorating on Christmas Eve. Mixed-results are of pleasure and smiles from students in higher up seats in lecture hall, and dismay with frowns from Maggie and students sitting in lower lecture theatre seats and near to me. Christmas Eve celebration is later held outside in the college's centre court where we all are offered sparklers and leader of event, Tiffany, stands near with couple friends lighting all sparklers.

Later returning to my apartment from lighting sparklers oldest son, Mark, video calls and said, "Do you have your passport?"

I said, "Yes. I return from Hangzhou with passport 02 December."

Registration of Foreign Resident Permit is with two return trips to Hangzhou from Tongcheng, and five hour fast train trip. Twice since late arrival in Tongcheng in mid October, surprising travel schedule develops after new government process of acquiring necessary authentications for Z Visa before arriving in China. Difficulties with control of passport evolve from travel time for foreigner registering for permit. Two five hour return trips to Hangzhou to leave passport for thirty day evaluation after arrival in Tongcheng are late in term in mid October, due to application procedures before arrival. Returning trips to Hangzhou, home of employer to register and retrieve passport, in mid November, are required. Regulations are new and months later in March 2018, register as a foreigner for Foreign Resident Permit both in Anqing, government city of Anhui, an hour away by car and then in Tongcheng, the city to work in as foreign English teacher. The Foreign Resident Permit allows foreigners permission to work in China for extended months in contracts. In video call with Mark describe Christmas celebration with lighted sparklers in evening's darkness under palm trees sharing with students.

Mark, foreign teacher for over decade many years in South Korea advising before arriving in China said, "Foreigner must never give up passport under any condition including while staying in hotels."

Exits and Entrances Bureaus in Hangzhou, Anqing and Tongcheng, police units supervising foreign residents, evaluate passports and documents.

"Mom, you are living the dream to be paid for two months of holiday," said Mark in video visit in second Christmas in Tongcheng.

Most important Hangzhou employer adviser's advice from Lynn suggests returning to original location, Tongcheng, preferable in discussions of offer to return to China for second ten-month contract. Employer is responsible for applying on behalf of foreigner working in China for Work Permit from Bureau in Hangzhou. While studying teaching skills in Beijing in July 2017, the manager of the English as foreign language training school is advising the visiting foreign teachers the example of a foreign teacher ignoring his advice in detention four days for working in addition to the accurate Z Visa and Permanent Resident Permit.

College students leave the college for their homes shortly after 25th of December, and return to Tongcheng College in early March to resume their classes until end of June. Time allows for rest or exercise, and illustrate from memory with crayons packed into water bottles on reusable coffee paper filters preparing with emptying, washing and drying in previous term and save, or any reusable materials. papers brought with me. Holiday times are filled with sketching buildings and area around college's playground visible from daily walks at college playground in these weeks from January to March.

Soon in the next days early in holiday of 2017, text messages from Crystal are to go out for New Year's meal with college faculty, and Crystal will come to apartment to help to first attend student presentation at college's training room on sixth-floor of large academic buildings, and then to celebration supper. After agreeing to arrangement, Crystal comes to apartment to walk to cross street from apartment to event. We walk up six flights of stairs in building see in view from window in apartment. Maggie meets in hallway outside, and explain text messages with Crystal. Maggie's texts were of attending event with Maggie's friend's training school

Maggie said, "Police officers might try to reach me, and must answer Maggie's text messages."

Yet follow Maggie into training room, a large room with a high ceiling, a stage, and a computer screen like a movie theatre, and first time experience. On screen music and images are accompanying cast of Flight Attendant Certificate students performing on stage. An empty seat is available beside David, Dean of English Department. David is speaking to students in next seats. David, Maggie, Crystal, myself and Chinese teachers walk to nearby restaurant to College to meet president of college for our celebration meal.

APART FROM ENGLISH AS FOREIGN LANGUAGE CLASSROOM

Tongcheng's community park, with wide walking path, fills with local people circling around outer limits and lawns where kites are flown, children are with parents in playground nearby and groomed seasonal flower beds of variety of annual plants. Wide and narrow fountain on wall of flowing water is central location to see square dancing with girls and women dancing together by day or by night.

One evening in same spring of 2017, Maggie texts to accompany her to park as she plans to meet new male date, and asks for help and friendship and passenger riding on Maggie's e-bike driving down Longmian West Road on warm evening in early June. Later on casual walk in spring Maggie explains losing interest in boyfriend as man contacts two women working at same college.

During college festival holiday in this first spring February 2017, in Tongcheng when canteen is closed, walk down Longmian West Road to left of college's entrance gate to same fast food fair visiting first morning in Tongcheng with Annie and Sherlock, and stalls are filled with variety of cooking for sale to purchase all day like breakfast pancake stuffed with eggs and vegetables and fried Annie buys and enjoy. After walking back to college, male student approaching while sitting in sunshine on boulevard eating pancake inside college's front gate, asks to walk to same park nearby visiting in earlier weeks with Annie or Maggie. Student studies creative writing. In spring flower blossoming season our conversation is about colours of flowers, and agree. We leave college campus turning right to walk down Longmian West Road several blocks to cross busy street to street light to crosswalk to main gate to park instead of jay-walking to cross street as with both Maggie and Annie on separate times. We stroll through park discussing flowers and colours. On return walk to college, ask student to wait as will stop at vegetable market on corner to buy some fresh vegetables. Student brings out some change from his pocket to buy gift of potatoes. We continue walk to college and depart at college gate.

In April 2017, buy first very large mango size of small football from supermarket to celebrate birthday.

Mango costs thirteen yuan, and supermarket cashier calls male manager who said, "Do I want to buy fruit?"

"Of course. Yes," I said.

On college bench next to fenced community basketball tennis courts busy with players, in sunshine sit in view of college's front lawns with grove of palm trees to enjoy eating and tearing apart one very large mango. Many students, including Stephanie and Crystal, complain following year supermarket prices are too high, no bargain and same as nearby food markets. Shopping in supermarket in winter holiday are stories to students in classroom conversations of when canteen closes, and still shocking to students of foreign teacher's ability to manage. College students shop at nearby smaller shops for fruits to enjoy in dormitory rooms.

Fancy lacy dresses are common classroom looks from students in September 2016, and continue until end of second term in June 2017. After returning to Tongcheng Teachers College for second contract in October 2017, until July 2018, blue jeans are worn by both male and female students. Once in awhile a student will wear pretty lacy dress to class, and continue to be worn by students to class randomly in second year after returning to college. On Easter Sunday 2018, as leaving the canteen after breakfast of congee, and boiled eggs, small group of female students look dressed-up in dresses of cream or colours are leaving. On any Sunday clothes racks are filled with washed clothes in boundary outside canteen and near dormitories.

On one occasion in spring of 2018, near completion of my second contract walking towards canteen for evening meal, one familiar teacher and Maggie's colleague from participation with students in English Corners, is passenger on e-bike driven by her female colleague. They stop at dormitory for young women, and notice her wearing the worn-looking, trendy mangled jeans with tears.

Colleague is smiling and said, "Hello."

Student English Corner Event, food snack gift from student in Tongcheng College

Previous June 2017, Joanna arranges photo of our English Corner group taken in front of college's library, and emails copy to share with family. This Colleague's husband comes to take photo on the June day. Often invitations to lecture theatre classroom is where power point presentations, games, and prizes and balloons are organized by students leading college's English Corner events for freshman and sophomore English Major students. Maggie and this colleague are at these events and we sit together in front row of theatre seating to watch activities and games for both of two ten-month contracts at Tongcheng Teachers College. Events last one hour in early evening. Student assistants Joanna, from first contract in 2016 to 2017, or Crystal or Stephanie, from second contract in 2017 to 2018, chaperone walks to occasional events, and come to apartments to walk across college campus to lecture theatre. Students ask to participate, and leave events with balloons or holiday decorations, like gift of Halloween double bat headband. College groups hold events and sales at tables in college's main avenue. Students unknown offer gifts such as pretty fan for hot weather printed with image of apple, pink glitter long stem red rose pen, and pens that look like carrots.

During second contract in spring 2018, Tiffany and students hold English Corner meeting with smaller group of freshman students in classroom gathering in six-storey building housing most of classes or offices, and Crystal arrives at apartment to walk across wide expansive lawn from large academic buildings. Students begin to speak of their futures after college, and if college education offers hope for opportunities after completing studies. The English Corner monitor in second ten-month contract, Tiffany, is student monitor of one of two senior sophomore three year English Major classes and sharing in class in spring of 2018, she travels to Beijing during holidays with boyfriend and tours an Olympic stadium from recent Beijing Olympics. Tiffany explains in class she chooses her name from love of movie Breakfast at Tiffany's, with Audrey Hepburn, and dreams of travel to and work in New York. Tiffany wears shoulder length black hair and bangs. Tiffany is soft-spoken, polite and has facial skin white like porcelain. One Sunday in spring in Tongcheng while sitting eating in outdoor food market near college's front gate, Tiffany walks by, carrying a few shopping bags, and stops to buy food. She looks glamorous in this simple food fair.

In January 2018, after faculty restaurant meal and leaving restaurant, outside of front entrance Sue, a Business English instructor, stops to chat to discuss invitation to join her in classes outside college classrooms at local business but with approval of college administration. In our chat explain to Sue, David and college must agree, as Maggie is standing to our right. Sue explains class preparation for vocabulary she will assume, as request is to lead for conversations. Later David, apartment neighbour and supervisor, stops to speak outside our apartment building advising college approval in meeting with administration for foreign teacher to work on Saturdays at local company factory to teach English conversation skills. College is sending one English teacher, Sue, for instructing lower management staff grammar in speaking English as a Foreign Language. David will assure extra monetary payment of as much as five thousand Renminbi depending on number of visits to company. David explains college's faculty are beginning to advise and guide students to look for work in factories or companies with English as a working language.

On first class at company in schedule tour management offices, and as we reach one manager sitting at desk in his office smiling manager said, "Hello."

Our class of English as Foreign Language company's students tour desks for daily work and students explain their roles and work for company. The classroom is like a boardroom. A list of topics for discussion and role plays, chosen by these staff members, are introduced to me in both written and verbal explanations to practice with employees. The group's only female member makes me coffee on occasion with espresso machine that sits on boardroom's table. Tours of the offices and factory are chosen by students for lessons. The local company's staff explain nature of work at factory and head office in Taiwan.

In tour of the factory said, "What about difficulty in obtaining documents to open a factory in Tongcheng and from another place?"

Staff laugh. "Taiwan is province of China so company is able to open factory in Tongcheng," said leader of our factory tour.

Large floor of workers at machines is lit brightly and next to many desks is room with machine taking x-rays of finished products for security checking. Factory students explain together, job young woman demonstrates is lengthy twenty-hour shift and pays more. Factory is quieter on Saturday with fewer workers.

Company's students choose English names unique to their own beliefs. Seven, a sales representative, chooses a lucky number and Front, the company's accountant, is ambitious with encouragement from daughter to learn English speaking skills.

One of Front's favourite stories to speak English is about company's holiday celebration serving favourite food of tomatoes and scrambled eggs. Seven always sits to left and Front sits across boardroom table.

One Saturday morning a couple of sessions later, Seven shows photo of blonde, tanned white young woman sitting on a beach and said, "Picture is dream holiday and to see Western woman and his dream holiday."

After first lesson at the company, Seven and Front invite Sue and myself to evening meal at a hotel where people are signing in at main desk and private dining rooms are booked. Sue always meets in a vehicle at the college with driver, Seven, to attend English as Spoken-Business English language classes. Several times we share lunch together in company's canteen. The canteen is large with many tables and through double doors from kitchen is large field in back they explain is for growing vegetables for cooking in canteen. Large dormitories are adjacent to canteen where workers stay but pay rent and food fees.

Near close of term in June 2018, Saturday is sunny and warm and teachers Sue and I are invited by Front and Seven to nearby restaurant for lunch after last class.

As we are waiting for students to arrive Sue said, "New campus will open next May 2019, and college is building up in mountain area away from our location."

"Sounds great to hear," I said.

After class, Seven drives and and with Front drive to restaurant, a bright, modern restaurant nearby with many flowers, flowering trees, and fish aquarium. Ordering dish of fish is Front's preference, and Sue often chats in Chinese to both Seven and Front. Front attempts to teach Mandarin expression, as we laugh together seated at quiet booth table in corner amidst decorative flowers around our final formal class meeting.

Students from company arrange our final lesson. We meet at Tongcheng Teachers College gate to drive out of Tongcheng to nearby Environmental Park. At entrance to park we stop to get out of van with Sue, Seven and Front and members riding in second vehicle to view white blossoms of very large lotus fields nearby park's sign and main entrance. The park holds ancient tools and outdoor wood stoves they students and Sue explain are still in use in homes, or Sue's father's farm. Sue takes many photos. We sit down at outdoor covered large stoves near couple caged peacocks. Large stoves are cold and resemble large campground stoves at national parks in home-country. Together sitting outdoors, we sing a song from words taught as if in our English as foreign language class back at their business offices, "You Are My Sunshine." We sing together sitting around picnic tables underneath cover of outdoor cooking centre, and similar to parks before arriving at fancy Environmental Park restaurant, sitting like original caretaker's home near front gate, and lunch together.

What is more in our dining-room at Environmental Park Restaurant is first invitation to join in game at mahjong table for four players. Table is fitted with automatic tile dispensers with four players sitting in the restaurant and where I am taught by Seven assisting with moves of game.

STUDENTS IN ENGLISH AS FOREIGN TEACHER'S CLASSROOM

Online shopping is popular with students. During spring 2018, in my second contract in senior five year English major smaller class of seven students arrive in ten minutes rest and preparation time before class begins. Diana, who chooses name for Princess Diana and loves stories about sons of Diana in Royal Family, brings her package to class to open, as she shops online and picks up package on way to class from canteen's shipping office. Inside her package are her new canvas shoes and free socks she lifts out of packaging and holds up to admire. Most students pick up packages at the new location of second shipping office on second floor of canteen opening during my second year working at Tongcheng Teachers' College. One main shipping office for sorting and sending is in glassed-in building at college's gate sharing with college's photocopying service.

Twenty-five minutes of final minutes of forty-five minute classes are speaking practice schedule for four to six students to stand in groups in corner or spacing in groups around the classroom to discuss foreign teacher's lesson topics. For example in five year English Major classes topic lesson is built around topics of clothing or fashion choices. After teaching and practising lesson vocabulary for fashion choice is topic for one female student, Jessica, to speak English to comment on recent style of torn blue jeans. Jessica explains stylish jeans that are expensive, approximately three hundred. Jessica is tall, muscular and sits with her best friend, Cindy, side by side at front of class, and appear like leaders of class of fourteen with one male student.

Students try to take turns in speaking-time in groups for lesson, but will ask another student to continue on with their cell phone games. Classroom behaviour is disruptive with playing games on phones. Often in groups or sitting in desks students are found playing games on cellphones, and with request to speak on topic in group, students will ask any other student to continue on with their cell phone games. Classroom behaviour is disruptive with gaming, and issue shows increasing in use in class after returning to college and second ten-month contract in 2017. Attendance is regular and improving for all students in this Jessica's class of fourteen Five Year English Major students. These students start college at sixteen years of age. Often students express their confidence in English language skills and future employment as teachers, and often are in practicums at local training schools. Their English speaking skills in class are mixed with a lot of spoken Chinese as students speak to each other during class.

Classroom students' participation includes their own English words to speak English to each other, and to speak English in their turn to speak English in classroom circle conversations. Students in both five year and three year teaching certificates practice to become practice English teachers in training schools for young children with their teaching practice schedule arrangements from college instructors during terms.

After arriving in Tongcheng in September 2016, fireworks is heard blasting off in daytime. While walking with student assistant, Joanna describes fireworks representing deaths or marriages. During classes, loud bangs of firework noise become distractions for everyone, and try to raise teaching voice to speak over fireworks, loudly in class to be heard, or wait few minutes. Request from Joanna, student assistant is to speak loud to project my voice across large classroom of forty to fifty students. During freshman class before our noon hour lunchtimes and two hour break, in autumn in 2016, waiting for few minutes until noise of fireworks stops is improving managing fireworks banging noise and distracting while students are speaking or listening to the instructions for conversation tasks. Daily fireworks look like sparklers bouncing off of tall college buildings into sky. Sometimes playground visitors position and explode fireworks at base or on Tongcheng's mountain or witness while walking at playground exploding from near local Buddhist temple that sits in view of the college's playground. Aspects of returning to Tongcheng for second ten-month contract to Tongcheng's college are the experience of daily fireworks disappearing.

During first or second ten-month contracts of 2016 to 2018, introducing each lesson with review of learning English names for students in classroom discussions is by distributing name cards students write English names to use to share their conversations and introductions to classrooms of students. Students are asked to identify themselves in class from hearing English name calling for attendances and conversations. Students choose original names with English letters.

In one sunny afternoon day in June 2018, Joyce, student in English Major five year certificate program and graduating soon, runs up to chat as returning to apartment from lunch at canteen on college's main avenue said, "I am accepted into university. in China. I am grateful for hard work in classroom experiences in English as a Foreign Language class."

Joyce choosing prior name to speak English that resembles Chinese rock star and translates the Chinese name into English loves her new name said, "Joyce is name I am glad I choose for English name easy to introduce myself with in entrance interview to university."

Joyce's best friend in English as foreign language classes keeps Chinese rock star name, instead of changing from rock star's name like Joyce, and stops while passing and walking to the library in June said, "Hello. I am going to library to write test."

"Good luck. Do well. You are very capable," I said.

Joyce's friend said, "I am studying to pass tests at the library to find a job in a local training school."

They are both local students from Tongcheng attending Tongcheng Teachers' College.

During final weeks of classes in June 2018, Dean of Physics walks into classroom of five year English Major students said, "Do you know the students are playing games?"

I said, "Yes. Students are attempting the lesson."

One female student, Cindy, and a best friend to Jessica, runs to back of classroom when Dean of Physics walks into class interrupting English as foreign language lesson. Cindy has thick long hair and is confident in her English speaking skills.

"I continue with Spoken English lesson and ask students to attempt English speaking exercises despite students playing games on their cellphones and students ask each other to manage their phone and game to participate in lessons, and another student takes over games on their classmate's phone," I said.

Later in mid June 2018, memo and survey for students from college expressing concern for students by students playing games in class. The memo is sent in research-style requesting student comments.

One student brings survey to English as foreign language class said, "All classes at college are affected by students using cellphones in class to play games. Solutions are suggestions from students and include: prohibiting phones from the classroom, disciplining students who play games as these students are distractions to other students and evicting students from class for game playing."

In between ten to eleven-thirty morning class of forty students, three year English Major certificate sophomore student is receiving text messaging in morning class. The journal notes are recorded in evening while resting after class.

Deciding to Leave Journal from China No.26.

She began to cry and no explanation was provided from the other students as I went to the students desk to ask. This student is very pleasant and always with a serious boyfriend on Campus or in the Canteen who say hello to the Foreign Teacher. She often walks with me in the mid afternoon after classes on Fridays at the College's playground sport track, has a steady boyfriend she introduced to me in the Canteen. The couple are often seen walking together on Campus. Later on a Friday mid afternoon as we walked together, the student mentioned her Mom was very ill with cancer, and was the news sent to her as she sat in class crying. As the term ends, she sits in the classroom with a friend after class ends and seems to confuse the College Monitor arriving to lock the door and check the classroom who must ask them to leave as all students have left class. I took a few minutes to pack up my notes and textbook. Maulo

In the second next year in winter holiday in January 2018, attend private training school with David's, Dean of English, wife managing. We sit side by side. College student is employed now at the training school and is managing young training school students preparing to perform beside our seats. Front of room is set aside for students taking turns.

I said, "Hello. It's good to see you working here. Congratulations."

"Very sad news student's Mom dying," David said.

The student is speaking to children she is managing.

More male students are enrolled in October 2018, and building of apartment from previous year is converted to male dormitory. Early in morning large groups of male students are heard and see running together outside apartment window at six am.

In 2016, "Ten percent of students at Tongcheng Teachers College are male," David said.

As English Major Department enrolment is lower in second ten-month contract, Maggie said, "Eighteen classes are schedule for all teachers, and add Flight Attendant Certificate classes to new foreign teaching evening schedule."

After returning in October 2017, Hotel Management classes continue in schedule, as in first 2016 contract, and new very large classes with students in Tourism Certificate is popular with higher enrolment than in first ten-month contract. Japanese Major students are added to round up English as foreign language teaching class schedule to eighteen weekly classes.

Meeting in January 2018, in his apartment waiting for building manager's help with apartment key as lock myself out of the apartment, David said, "Enrolment in the English Major Certificates is not much from the English Major Department."

Enrolment in English as Foreign Language classes is decreasing from forty to twenty-five students in freshman classes. Number of males in Tourism Vocational Certificate classes in English as a Foreign Language is much higher than in English Major classes.

Romance is common among students, and dormitories are supervised by guards and faculty teachers doing check-in to student dormitories at nine o'clock. On one occasion, Maggie asks to join her to check in at one dormitory for female students as she is helping her colleague who is absent. Student dormitories for first year students are crowded with three sets of bunk beds for up to six students in each dormitory room. Near mid June students are becoming sophomore students and transition to moving-up to dormitories with more amenities with fewer students in dormitories before ending the school year in June. Students are organized by dormitory adult supervisors to walk together to new dormitory locations. Sophomore students live in male, female or co-ed dormitory buildings.

After arriving in Tongcheng later in term in October 2017, one afternoon, "Can we sit together?" Elinor said at canteen.

Elinor sits across canteen table, and canteen server walks pass as nod in agreement. Later after more meetings in canteen, Elinor offers thank-you beef tofu snacks made in her local area and accept.

Elinor, freshman student joining to often walk together at playground or share meals in canteen said, "New dormitory-room is very pleasant with single bed, desk, built in shelving, private bathroom and heating. I got help from teacher from fear of lower bunk and upper bunk roommate with stacking packages on bed above to move from freshman dormitory."

Elinor visits local national historic Confucian temple with classmate on Sunday for activity. Grandparents visit her for their first time visit to Elinor at college, and to Tongcheng, and Elinor takes her grandparents to local bookstore. While walking downhill from walking at college playground later in spring 2018, Elinor passes with her visiting mother near student dormitories in term two, and smiles are exchanged. Elinor's mother offers and accept same bag of snack tofu from their local area bringing to visit and accept. After arrival in October 2017, Elinor joins me for meals occasionally in the canteen, where we meet for the first time.

Female students share their dormitory-rooms with other female students, and male students share with male students. Some buildings include both male and female students on one floor. All students hang their laundry out windows on racks that are lowered and raised for laundry drying.

At end of terms in both winter and spring, garbage bins are overflowing with students' personal belongings like clothes, shoes and personal effects. Mountains of garbage are collected by man with cart he pulls. Local college and Tongcheng adult residents sort through piles of student belongings salvaging for their own use. Local shipping company comes onto campus to assist students to ship their personal clothes and any items they want to take with them on their return to their homes. Larger than garbage bag size olive green bags are sold for packing and weighing outside student dormitories.

In June 2017, deciding to use shipping service being offered to students ship suitcase of winter clothing and gifts from family in same dark olive green bags to employer's offices in Hangzhou to store over summer months until returning to China without employer's defining plans with college for return to Tongcheng College. Day before departure from first of two ten-month contracts, gift packages of tea from college ship from college's shipping office overseas to family. Joanna, student adviser in first year, asks her male friends to help with translations with clerks and at shipping offices located at college gate. Male students carry luggage from apartment for shipping to employer in Hangzhou for storage, and walk from hillside to shipping office at college's front gate, and with gifts of tea to ship to family overseas final day in Tongcheng.

ENGLISH AS FOREIGN LANGUAGE TEACHER

During term two of second ten-month contract, walk to college's shipping office at college's gate to ship ahead heavy, large suitcase and clothes-drying rack. On Friday afternoon May 2018, after lunch and college's daily rest between twelve and two after lunch is when no classes are scheduled. The shipping office is located at the campus gate. Through path between palm trees, walk to enjoy surroundings to arrange to ship suitcase filling with small gifts from college students, faculty gifts containers of green tea and heavier clothes from winter. The suitcase is difficult to manage at very long, wide and steep staircase to waiting-room at Hefei Fast train station for the leg-of-the-trip from Tongcheng to Shanghai, and travel between two airports after arriving on fast train in Shanghai.

Meanwhile keynotes to shipping ahead are with help from sophomore student, Joy, to translating instructions to college shipping clerks.

Only by chance do we meet at college gate location of shipping office, and speaking-up Joy said, "I can offer English translations to shipping clerks."

Small shipping office is with wall to wall and to ceiling curtained windows and run with two younger male clerks speaking only Chinese or local dialect.

"Thank you. Your help is appreciated. I ship drying rack to reduce electricity from electric clothes-dryer in permanent home, after departing," I said.

Joy walks back to apartment through palm tree park or meets later at shipping office, and negotiates with shipping clerks.

Joy said, "I am surprised to know of electric dryers in homes. Friend attends Ottawa University tells me she can even wear t-shirt in winter inside from heating in dormitory."

During first year at Tongcheng Teachers College in English as Foreign Language freshman personal introduction class Joy said, "I won scholarship to university from same country you arrive from but scholarship pays one-half of education tuition costs. Scholarship is still available next year."

"Congratulations," I said.

Soon Maggie tells Joy's plan to leave Tongcheng Teachers College to attend foreign university are concerns for Maggie and colleagues to speak to Joy about feeling content to be attending college in Tongcheng.

"All students must write qualifying test to register at Tongcheng Teachers College," Maggie said.

Returning to Tongcheng Teachers College October 2017, find Joy begins to participate in college life and enjoys volunteering in student's union.

Shipping clerk and Joy come to apartment after meeting second time to examine suitcase and carry suitcase to shipping office. Two young men weigh suitcase in shipping office.

Joy said, "Return to apartment for more clothes and return later to the shipping office to stuff more clothes into same suitcase."

Many text messages are sent from Joy to shipping clerks and to her foreign teacher. While sharing our walk from shipping office through park of palm trees nearby to campus Joy said, "My Chinese teacher tells me to get more output and helping is more time to practice speaking English and to translate English to shipping clerks." Later in final text Joy said, "Shipping clerks negotiate for twenty-five percent reduction for costs with Shanghai company."

Total cost to ship suitcase and drying rack is four thousand yuan.

On the other hand after returning to Tongcheng months earlier October 2017, walk up main avenue to playground, busy with student fun competing events, and are met with welcomes from new and known students.

"Hello," said students.

After crossing playground to several tables in line, student monitor offers gift of candy bag from their freshman table that is competing in annual games of races and relays. Female student is active in student union business, and meet her boyfriend at student union dinner in restaurant later during winter vacation in December 2017.

Maggie said, "Students suggest to invite guest to join to student union dinner."

Maggie is student union's staff adviser. We sit together visiting after meal as long as possible at small round table on second-floor of heated restaurant.

Yet at completion of autumn term in December 2017, in second of two ten-month contracts and after returning to Tongcheng in October 2017, Crystal texting said, "Can students come to apartment with gifts?"

Sophomore of four freshman students visit apartment.

Donna said, "Gift of protein is for health. Often mothers make soy protein milk for their babies as milk is scarce"

Other gifts include bag of cut bamboo sticks and said, "How are sticks eaten?"

Classmate Amy, second year sophomore student, demonstrating starts biting off end of stick of bamboo to chew for sweetness. Amy is recently meeting and walking together at playground to practise her English-speaking skills. Amy comes to meet on quiet Sunday morning one day earlier to give her hand-drawn poster size crayon drawing coloured on paper like packing paper of large Santa Claus.

"I colour picture night before," Amy said.

"Come here," I said to Amy, and show poster hanging over old calendar in apartment. "I enjoy your effort at colouring Santa Claus. I will be keeping the Santa Claus poster in my belongings when I depart Tongcheng."

"Will you be staying for second term?" Donna said.

"I will be staying until June," I said.

On the other hand, washing clothes is dependent on weather and in spring one student coming late to class said, "Washing clothes."

In the springtime 2018, more casual and relaxed confident students are evolving in Spoken English classes with classroom expectations to speak only English after entering classroom. Politeness between students except in classroom choice of behaviour and speaking Chinese in class is thought as distracting. During this particular freshman class, the student who arrives late to the classroom apologizes for arriving late in English words to class due to an opportunity she has to wash her clothes. As the sunny weather is appreciated, the chance to enjoy the relationship between the weather and washing clothes in an English conversation is an experience for us all to share. The student, who speaks with her apology for lateness, appears caring for personal duties with understanding from everyone in the classroom.

"In China, laundry is dependent on weather," Maggie said. "Laundry duties must coordinate with sunny weather as only method for drying clothes."

Some residents use a washing rock in a college location behind auditorium and below playground to beat and wash clothes while kneeling. On a spring hike in 2017, with Maggie outside of Tongcheng and nearby hydro plant in shallow river shore, a man is beating clothes with washing stick in water. Most neighbours of building during second contract in 2017, do as learn to do and hang clothes on their own apartment balcony after washing in a machine inside their apartment on drying rack. Balcony windows can open or close but the sunny weather shining into the balcony dries the clothes sometimes taking more than one day. The balcony is visible to all students and faculty from the roadway.

GREEN MOUNTAIN AT TONGCHENG TEACHERS COLLEGE

College avenue from college's main gate extending uphill past dormitories to top of hill with playground next to mountain is next to large lagoon and nearby to second large multi-storey music building. Fishing from shore of lagoon is common site and small vegetable fields are grown on the banks on main college avenue and across from playground. Tongcheng's mountain is filled with family tombs spread out mostly in one section above college's playground and with many paths for hikers. Encouraging words from David and Maggie in first meeting are air is very clean in Tongcheng from proximity to green mountain.

In February 2017, of first ten-month contract, sophomore student, Ánnie, and beginning to tutor is telling as we view mountain from open air kitchen of first apartment, "Last year try hiking mountain with friend but find experience walking past tombs very frightening."

Joanna, student assistant walking together on a racing track at the playground first month September 2016, in Tongcheng said, "Never go hiking on mountain as wild dogs live in mountain and are dangerous."

After returning to Tongcheng Teachers College and during second ten-month contract year next October 2017, nearby mountain is closed to students for hiking. Large dormitory at end of main college roadway past playground and below mountain near college's playground houses only female students. These students often walk together in late afternoons at playground.

One afternoon female student, who joins to practice speaking English while walking together at playground said, "Students live in fear of spirits on mountain."

JOURNAL NOTES from TONGCHENG COLLEGE ENDING EFL (ENGLISH AS FOREIGN LANGUAGE) CONTRACT

JUNE 24, 2017

My location in China will change but the Dean responsible for teachers, David, invites me with an invitation from

Maggie in the canteen, to his relative's training school. As I enjoy meeting new people and like being an English as Foreign Language teacher, I accept.

My student assistant, Joanna, is also to attend and will provide transportation instructions. We are supposed to tour Old Street. We leave the college at eight am. in a white car and pick up a fourth passenger. The school's flashing lights announce this event of a foreign English teacher's visit to the training School.

The training school flashing lights advertise a speech will be held. The school was a thirty minute drive to Kongcheng. Sixteen students, nine girls and seven boys ages eight to twelve approximately greet me and we climb stairs to the classroom. Cold water bottles are distributed to the guests and my introduction completed. My brief introduction of two or three sentences is followed with a free speech activity of students to teacher by raising a hand to ask the visiting foreigner any question. Every student is encouraged to have this chance by their regular Chinese teacher. My conversation with each participating student lasts for one, two or three questions and answers. We take a break and students push their desks to the walls on either side and Joanna leads them in a game. The game instructs each student to name themselves by their favourite fruit names seems to be an objective. No pictures or flash cards are used. The game has difficulty ending as the students are good at the game. The boys seem to win or a tie and the game ends.

The relative of David who owns the school records the question and answer conversations between myself and students. Maulo Time 09:00 to 10:00

We take a few photos. I am invited to walk to the Old Street. I enjoy the walk and view the newer store fronts mostly empty with seventy-five per cent vacancy. A few people are in the street. One human taxi walks quickly past with a Chinese woman, Granma and boy child. I am a curiosity to some.

We arrive at the location, where the training school teacher has described the streets as one thousand years old. The streets are covered in very large smooth rocks, most minimum size is ten inches by sixteen to twenty inch sizes I guesstimate. Another Chinese woman joins to make a group of four tourists visiting Old Street. We are not required to pay as the training school has provided costs. Walking through the streets seems quiet.

1. We visit the ancient school.

The training school teacher is the tour guide as her English is fair and Joanna can translate. The ancient classes were held in the bricked area in front of an attractive two storey building, ie. A nice looking house. I ask about a porch to the right built in concrete with an open circular door approximately six times ten feet. The porch outside the building was the teachers' sleeping area. The inside is the traditional home with an office to the right and left. A doorway to back leads to stairs and square concrete sunken bed to collect water. The roof is left open in the back to promote drying of the walls in heavy subtropical rain.

2. We visit the Prefect Mansion

The huge home is divided into large rooms across the building. There are chairs to rest and a large mantle with a mantle clock. I look at all the scrolls of paintings featuring scenes from the countryside of rivers, mountains, and people in various activities. One image of a man and a horse and a man and a large hoe-like tool over his shoulder can still be experienced in modern China except for the horse and rider. I wander through a second room to the back. In the middle between each section is a room on either side that look like large bedrooms or dining rooms. The second large room has closed off staircases on each side and in each corner are two large rooms, approximately twenty by thirty feet that may have been kitchen preparation rooms. The ceiling is twenty-five feet high approximately, however the explanation is the mansion is said to have a second floor that was removed in restoration. The Tongcheng Prefect had five daughters.

3. We visit the Military Station.

I enjoy this building as I have read and enjoyed a variety of Chinese fiction and non fiction military accounts. The room is large housing agriculture tools for working the soil. One wide steel tool with singular claws looks like a cultivator. Around the walls are straw baskets and one straw hat. (Sampan?). The training school guide follows me to the back room. Our fourth tour friend, who speaks no English, provided a lot of the information. The large square basin with open ceiling gathers the rain and the square concrete opening creates the drain. In the middle of the two basins is an attractive small stone insert twenty by twenty inches, is square, the other round. The room has a stairway to the right to an upstairs sleeping area for resident and a small balcony above the basin. Someone walking into the room would be visible from the balcony above.

4. We visit the Ginkgo Hall.

The tour guide explains the Hall was for military people and was destroyed by fire in the 1800's. All that is left is a rectangular concrete arch. The park like lot is decorated with plastic crafted windmills in multiple colours.

5. We visit the art and craft Gallery.

I ask to see the pictures as no one is interested. Inside on the walls are framed images of country scenes of people dressed in heavier clothes with tools that could be fishing tools. The scenes are all completed by paper toll in muted colours, ie. brown, beige, black. Two hundred and sixty-five and two hundred and ninety yuan are range of sale prices. The gallery manager comes to show us the flag or banner in a glass covered display case of the Titanic movie stars, Winslet and deCaprio meeting each other.

6. We stop for food.

The specialty in the restaurant is steamed dumplings with rice, rice and meat, chicken or beef. The manager-waitress brings us a teapot and cups and a plate of dumplings. The fourth school tourist takes a large cucumber out of her purse, breaks it in half, and reaches across the table to give me the other half. Everyone enjoys a dumpling and the plate is almost empty when a second plate of dumplings is brought. I begin to eat them enjoyably and three styro-foam containers to go are brought to table. The teatime was paid in advance.

7. We walk through some souvenir tables.

They suggest a fan of silk with a painting of flowers a good choice. Ten yuan is cost but say, "I have no room in suitcase.

8. We take our time leaving and can enjoy the display of large posters of local famous people. One I recognize as the local and famous opera star of the homei opera, Lei Fang On the walk leaving, a male basket weaver can be seen showing the craft, and a desk for an older male on a stage shows him painting Chinese letters in large black paint with brush onto a fan.

9. The three other tourists in my training school group take photos with their cameras and Joanna promises to share a couple with me by email.

10. We leave Old Street as a car has arrived to drive us back but we end going to a restaurant for lunch. The restaurant is small on first floor with a bar at back and two or three tables to the right. I am asked to lead up the narrow aggregate covered stairs and we reach a bright and cheerful dining room with sliding privacy doors and air conditioning. Green tea is served. We wait a few moments and the driver and the training school owner arrive to host the lunch. The driver explains he and the training school owner are a couple. Goose with tofu is main course, soy green beans, local steamed shrimp, greens steamed (spinach) white fish in large pieces (extremely good; steamed). White rice and noodles cooked in the table heated pot are last choices. Orange juice is served from two litre plastic bottle.

11. We leave restaurant.

On the drive back, we stop in an area of newer store fronts or shops but all seem empty. The garage-like door to one opens. We walk through the concrete room. A pool table covered sits to the left. Out the back door, a large farmyard appears. To the right is a chicken pen with six to twelve smaller chickens with their red caps and two large white geese (or ducks). We walk down the steep path to the vegetable garden filled over five acres approximately. Mature corn, very tall cucumber vines, and large radicchio leaves are picked. There is a fenced pond area where the fowl can visit by walking through an opening and down the steep slope.

I said, "Garden?"

Tthey all laugh. "Gardens refer to flowers. Field is tended by the driver."

12. We arrive back at Tongcheng Teachers College at 13:45, Maulo June 25, 2017

Gifts of cucumbers lunch partners pick are given at apartment where good-byes are shared while departing their vehicle driven by husband of training school and gardener. Cucumbers from the field are eaten whole, unsliced and put into apartment refrigerator in preparation for packing into lunch for fast train departing Anhui in next few days to travel to Shanghai and flight departing to Beijing.

PART THREE

FOREIGN TEACHER'S APARTMENTS

Text messages and phone call are from Tiger, Hangzhou employer's representative, day after arrival in Tongcheng in September 2016. Tiger takes taxi together to fast train station in Hangzhou and buys ticket to travel to Tongcheng.

Tiger said, "You must live in apartment. You must leave hotel."

Second day of stay in hotel in Tongcheng, walk to David's office on third floor of academic building to speak to David, Dean of English, sharing Tiger's instructions. David is sitting at desk in back of crowded small office.

I said, "Soon I must be able to live in apartment."

His assistant, Mr. Ye, who sits near doorway to this small office said, "Step back."

A young female is also sitting at desk on my left.

David said, "Apartment is almost ready in few days from cleaning and preparation."

"Thank you," I said, and leave their office to return to hotel.

Female police officer is behind front desk on my return to hotel speaking and checking with desk clerk's hotel register.

I said, "*Ni hao*"

Desk clerk smiling said, "*Ni hao.*"

Turning to immediate left walk to hotel elevator in pleasant hotel lobby with jade statues in front of large lobby window. Same female stout five foot ten police officer later will interview me in pleasant fashion twice at Tongcheng Bureau to transfer two Permanent Resident Permits from Anqing to Tongcheng.

Moving into apartment next day is with help from sophomore female college student assistant, Joanna, my college adviser, Maggie, and at least three more college students. Everyone arrives at my hotel room to carry heavy black suitcase and black canvas bag from hotel, and I wear backpack and shoulder bag with personal papers. Advice from family overseas is with gift of wide beige cloth pocket with zipper on plastic belt wearing passport in belt next to skin around waste with passport and cash converted into Chinese Renminbi at bank before travel overseas. In my first introduction in hotel room to Joanna, my new student assistant, give Maggie and Joanna each lapel pin from my hometown before we leave hotel to depart together.

Across street from hotel, college gate, wide with metal accordion style closing, opens for cars and people where uniformed guards monitor from guard house and outside their doorway. When first driven into view of college a two days earlier concrete archway appears above college gate. Large archways in front of schools or colleges will become common to see throughout at schools or colleges.

Couple days earlier, David, Dean of English, who comes with Maggie to meet trip from Hangzhou at Hefei fast train station said, "There is our college."

Our group crosses busy street from hotel to walk through this gate to round boulevard with huge rock engraved in green Chinese letters. Turning left, we walk uphill and climb interior concrete stairs to apartment on corner of fourth floor of five-story building. Outdoor covered balcony to apartment doorway is six-feet wide with same ceramic white tiles as inside apartment and leads from building's enclosed stairwell past former dormitory rooms to apartment. Balconies with similar roofs run entire lengths of walls from one wide zigzag style indoor concrete stairs on interior corner entrance with one staircase to floors from ground level. Close distance away from balconies library windowed offices in view is my daily walk. One walking bridge connecting dormitory building to library is pathway for residents on second floor.

With students lining up on exterior balcony, Maggie opens with key locked steel door to porch area to walk together through sliding door leading to kitchen with wall to wall sliding windows. Students open tall door on right to lead to double bed made-up with bright linens and quilts college provides to create warm welcome. Students help to tour apartment, and carry luggage to bedroom. Maggie shows how to open and lock apartment's front door, hands-over apartment key and students and Maggie leave apartment.

"Dean of English, David, holds only other key," Maggie said.

Outdoor covered balcony to apartment doorway is six-feet wide with same ceramic white tiles as inside apartment and leads from building's enclosed stairwell past former dormitory rooms to apartment. Balconies with similar roofs run entire lengths of walls from one wide zigzag style indoor concrete stairs on interior corner entrance with one staircase to floors from ground level. Responsibility is with Maggie for information sharing between college administration.

"Empty dormitory rooms will be soon occupied with Chinese college teachers hanging laundry or cooking who find bargain of free rent after discovering foreign English teacher is allowed to occupy apartment," said Maggie.

Neighbour and faculty teacher living in rooms on same fourth floor is permanent resident of Hefei, and where her husband continues to keep their home. She takes two dormitory rooms at corner beside stairwell to fourth floor. As their doorways are often open, we meet often arriving or leaving apartments. One dormitory room is for cooking and second dormitory room is for instructor, her small infant child and mother, who helps instructor with child care. Either teacher's mother or teacher become friendly to share greetings.

College on a misty day

EMPLOYERS

Employer's foreign adviser, Lynn, emailing before arrival to explain directions for after flight arriving in Shanghai. Lynn writes to take Long Bus four hours south to Hangzhou to meet Lynn due to security for fast train and international G-20 event in Hangzhou, and to email Lynn after arrival in Hangzhou or Shanghai. At Shanghai Pudong international airport, before reaching the luggage carousel, small table advertises wifi with woman standing behind. Few customers in front near table are speaking to sales person. Long bus signs direct passengers to walk lengthy distance to bus station where tickets are sold by cashiers. After getting in line to ticket wicket, bus stop guide checking line asks for my destination.

"Hangzhou," I said.

"Hangzhou?" said female guide in correct pronunciation.

Guide tells correct amount for bus ticket to Hangzhou, and for this reason take renminbi cash out of money belt wearing abroad on waste with passport abroad to pay cashier. Three thousand Chinese renminbi cash is Lynn's advice to bring. Guide continues to stand nearby as buying bus ticket at wicket, and then with guide's arm directions go outside, walk through glass to open double doorway to where another man sits at desk with security guards around and asks for passport. Seated long bus male clerk is sitting at desk outside and is taking look at passport photograph to compare, looking at me and motioning to board smaller bus behind on left nearby sitting waiting in sunshine on very hot day in Shanghai August 2016.

Although bus ride on this old bus is hot in humid weather, and we pass by towers of apartments leaving Shanghai in groups resembling dominoes. Four hours pass to relax alone in double seat arriving in Hangzhou outside restaurant as darkness descends.

To email Lynn of arriving decide to go inside restaurant, and at order counter said, "Wifi?"

Clerk shakes his head. A customer sitting nearby said, "Email is okay."

Though leave through restaurant rear door with large suitcase, canvas bag, backpack and shoulder bag. Standing in darkness outside behind restaurant is close to subway entrance with boarded sides. Since seems best to ask young male for help as he departs outside subway entrance. He speaks English and offers to phone his Russian friend. They invite me to Russian's home.

"Thank you," I said, and bring out Ipad stored in backpack by this time, "For email and do you have wifi?"

Young man is understanding requests deciding to offer his own internet address to add his address to iPad to email Lynn. Email is sent. In minutes Lynn's assistant comes through boarded entrance to subway to meet and after waiting inside subway station. We depart and Lynn's assistant asks to walk to same bus stop where departing long bus deciding on taxi to downtown Hangzhou and hotel to stay four days in hotel. Assistant checks on reservations with hotel clerks, clerks check passport and hotel clerks issue buffet breakfast tickets and hotel room-key.

"Miss complimentary breakfast buffet next morning due to medical tests," said Lynn's assistant.

Above hotel elevators to multi-storey modern hotel is Santa Claus picture and take elevator to floor of clean, modern air-conditioned room, double bed and with three piece bathroom.

More specifically Lynn arranges for medical tests in morning for myself and male foreign teacher and wait outside for Lynn and we walk together with new male foreign teacher to large international medical building. Foreigners wait in large waiting room and complete medical tests including weight, blood pressure, eye-sight and blood tests in rooms nearby on-the-spot. Male foreign teacher stays with his girlfriend who is foreign English teacher in Hangzhou and where he will stay on to teach. A lot of military personnel are guarding entrances we walk past and large stores with big and some familiar signs are visible behind plywood temporary barriers. Later we share lunch together in modern small restaurant with bakery, Lynn's treat and suggestion. Lynn helps choose from lunch choices in glass cases and pays cashier. To return to hotel, Lynn helps to take subway train with more than usual security for G-20 conference in crowded subway station, and points out lighted map with green lights appearing above our moving subway train seats to guide passengers on correct stop to depart subway.

Lynn said, "All residents of Hangzhou must leave city four countryside to enable high security for G-20."

"Where do they go?" I said.

"Most can visit other family in countryside, or anywhere," Lynn said.

In multi-storey mall across narrow street from hotel, large restaurant with patio and security guards walking among tables is easy to visit, eat french fries and drink coffee, Restaurant sits on corner to inside entrance to large mall with patio. In centre of urban mall are very wide tiled open air walkways and outdoor mall displays. During four days will buy french fries and coffee and eat both inside and outside on patio.

On quiet Sunday morning next day return to mall to browse and to find open drugstore. Clerk helps and is encouraging with price to buy hair colouring products from drugstore to cover hair in darker colour and extra products for months after.

Sunday evening return to mall and wander in opposite direction to eat in noodle-style restaurant where staff try to convince their food is too hot. Selection is made and find booth in restaurant, and take out new vintage soft mustard wallet with paisley lining to stare at and celebrate arriving. In next booth young males eat but ignore foreigner. Noodle restaurant is busy with customers most days, and another time eat in local Hangzhou family-style restaurant in mall.

Yet following year contract demands returning to Hangzhou in October 2017, and same hotel, and with travel with two more trips to Hangzhou to apply for Permanent Resident Permit.

Maggie said, "I am surprised of security guards in restaurant."

Nevertheless in August 2016, in mid-afternoon with free personal time in Hangzhou, take short walk from hotel in Binjang District through streets to riverbank. Huge statue of Silver Dragon towering forty feet overlooks Qiantang River and stroll about quiet city pond across from statue. Large yellow two-storey building similar to restaurant, club or tea house sits along riverside street a few hundred feet from Silver Dragon. Returning to riverbank near darkness next day is spectacle to explore lights of G-20 international conference appearing on riverbank across Qiantang River to downtown. Many men and women and families are photographing these vibrant evening lights spelling out G-20.

While training next day in employer's downtown office where foreign teachers on our break sit in cubicles one male foreign teacher who works in Hangzhou year before said, "I move from South Korea where cost of living is too high and after four months work costs in China are improvement. My apartment is near mall and river and in evening on occasion walk to riverside's green pathway to area where crowd of square dancing occurs each evening open to public and join in dancing once in awhile.

On first morning in Hangzhou as wait outside hotel for Lynn, teacher is outside hotel arguing with employer's representative, Tiger, said "I am not going anywhere until my stuff stored in my last location is brought to my new location here, including my e-bike."

In darkness stand nearby to watch square dancing in early evening at seven pm on Qiangtang riverbank and stroll down riverside's green belt with others and Chinese families enjoying G-20 light displays across river on riverbank and on buildings. Walking back to hotel pass exclusive men's shop still open and in distance with fibre lighting rising up apartment buildings and business towers to return to hotel before eight pm and is hotel staff's advice.

Next day Lynn and new foreign teachers struggle with applications for cellphone accounts at Hangzhou cellphone company's store in mall across street from hotel. In our group we walk to company's bank and open new bank accounts. Lynn suggests to deposit at least half our Renminbi cash brought with us from overseas, keeping smaller amount in cash-on-hand. Our personal cell phones brought with us are reviewed in employer's offices from where overseas interviews are held as problems develop.

In downtown employer's offices in Hangzhou from where first interview develops while overseas Lynn said, "I suggest you accept older cellphone to overcome problems with G3 Motorola cellphone bringing to China."

"Okay. Thanks. Shall I return this phone?" I said.

Lynn said, "No. Yours to keep."

One evening wait and sit in outer office into evening at Lynn's request. Around five in afternoon Lynn appearing said, "It's okay to depart to hotel."

Next day during afternoon of final day in employer's offices in Hangzhou Lynn said, "School, who interviews before departure to China cancels contract."

"What are their issues?" I said.

"Does not matter," said Lynn. "Two choices are there is this farther away place, a college, where request to work fifteen hours per week teaching conversational English is one choice or work short hour's distance from Hangzhou in middle school with work extra hours tutoring for payment to make lot more money and also return to visit us in Hangzhou?"

Before arriving in China headhunter calls March 2016, and said, "Are you interested in working in China in kindergarten?"

"No. I am able to work fifteen hours each week with young adults in conversational English," I said.

Request for immediate interview with headhunter's employer within hour is agreeable and offer evolves in next twenty-four hours to teach conversational English at college in China fifteen hours per week. During afternoon waiting in employer's offices in Hangzhou, and reviewing our contract find clauses to allow arbitration of any dispute and begin to decide on plans to proceed, either staying for holiday or travel to South Korea, as already in Asia. Hence accept Lynn's offer to teach English in conversations fifteen hours per week at Tongcheng Teachers College.

In truth months of preparation during quiet hours in evenings before arriving in China are writing free verses in four lines with one to two syllables for sharing on art hobbyist website in gallery of English as foreign language or English as second language poetry. Emotions, objects or actions in writing original four lines into free verses in one and two syllable words guide my belief to develop obscure qualities of learning to speak English in conversations with impressions of nature or emotions for example.

Before departing Hangzhou by fast train to Tongcheng employee-manager, Shirley, said, "Ask for college's schedule of school classes?"

Shirley is glancing as she walks with our group of foreign teachers to speak to me walking in sunshine after our lunch in restaurant in Hangzhou, Zhejiang three days after arriving in China before departing to Tongcheng, Anhui, in next province. In three days, all foreign teachers visit three locations of employer's Hangzhou training schools meeting teachers and learning teaching-tools for classroom management.

After one more night in Hangzhou hotel, Tiger meets out front to drive to fast train station, and for first experience on supersonic train travel at high speeds.

In taxi Tiger said, "Hangzhou has nine million people."

We are in huge crowd at station, and Tiger decides to run in front to buy tickets so asks to wait alone. Tiger returns and we go through security added for G-20 conference. Thick crowd winds around corners to entrance to train station. Tiger stays close to arrive at gate to train where he departs. Heavy black suitcase, bulging back-pack and small cloth carry-on are all mine to manage down flight of stairs to open-air deck to find correct fast train. After boarding attendant takes large suitcase to keep in entrance and exit to retrieve and store carry-on with back-pack between feet. In seat on left of window seat, young man sits and later asks about travel, of practising some English-speaking that is good, and offers water given from dispenser in paper cups. Retrieving Ipad from back-pack take many pictures of country-side in exciting venture to travel in China only known from news and books and to see sampans, bamboo groves or farmers planting in rice paddies.

In first evening of my arrival in Tongcheng during our supper together with David and faculty, Maggie is asking to walk with her to her office on campus after welcome supper. We walk in darkness crossing street through college's lighted gate and walk in avenues to climb interior stairs to darkened third-floor of college two-joined buildings with classrooms and offices. After we are seated in Maggie's office, Maggie is offering paper in her handwriting for schedule of classes on official college paper for English as foreign language classes.

"Please type out schedule and thank-you Maggie for schedule of classes," I said.

Day later and after receipt of typed schedule from Maggie, Ipad photograph of schedule is attached to email to Lynn, continuing to be foreign representative in Echo Education's office in Hangzhou while working in Tongcheng.

COLLEGE SECURITY

More specifically soon in one evening September 2016, in Tongcheng, after walking from playground back to first apartment at college at approximately five-thirty pm, car pulls up as I enter building doorway to building and first apartment.

Driver gets out of car and in English said, "Time is late to be outside."

Daily schedule to walk at playground adjusts to during daytime or before eating supper at four pm when canteen opens for evening meal.

Walking for exercise and relaxation at college's playground cushioned sport track, in mornings without classes or after classes in afternoon or after twelve to two pm rest, is familiar quiet routine most days. After returning to college in next October 2017, often choose to rest in apartment in early mornings without classes in schedule enjoying steamed buns for breakfast and purchasing from canteen day before to store in refrigerator when classes are later in day or in free-time in weekend taking more leisure.

In truth in daytime walk alone from apartments up main college street to playground after classes anytime before lunch or supper in canteen during either first and second years as English foreign language teacher meeting students, who may try to speak English to me. Students are coming and going from classes walking uphill or downhill on lengthy main avenue sharing free time together in playground or walking for afternoon rest to student dormitories.

At playground in autumn 2016, Joanna said, "Students enjoy free-time together until nine pm due to dormitory curfews walking together at playground, going to restaurants or eating at food-fair outside college gate down street from college. Taking bus once knife is stabbed into backpack on crowded bus and all identification is stolen."

After return to Tongcheng for second ten-month contract October 2017, discover small police station is set up on campus. Next door to apartment building in space below music school small office with police station sign is near apartment's walkway and across college street from grassy lawns, palm trees and two-adjoined salmon-white academic buildings. Seldom are police officers walking about college campus. One day walking to college gate, pass younger male police officer who seems to notice foreigner with his slight smile.

MAKING-A-HOME

On Christmas Day 2016, our first morning to visit and six years since he visits our family in homeland, after receiving Mark's text from his Tongcheng hotel stand near college gate and security guard house. Taxi stops, Mark gets out, runs towards me and hugs, and covers me around head with his arms for our happiness meeting in Tongcheng as guard watches nearby.

"We can go for walk," I said, and depart together to walk down Long Mian West Road and look at some lotions for wife Jin.

We shop at small store across from college gate to find "same Brands are identical to brand Jin uses in South Korea." Mark said.

Together stroll several blocks short distance down Long Mian West Road, turn right, cross busy intersection, walk another long block, and turn right past bank and past few smaller shops to Tongcheng supermarket. We walk into supermarket from concrete path or stairs, and through hanging plastic panels to main floor to check backpack and Mark's shoulder bag in supermarket locker in rows at back on main floor.

"Bring your own shopping bags for purchases is possible," I said.

Mark buys me eggs and bread for Christmas Day 2016. We walk together to college gate for Mark is leaving to hail a taxi to go to their hotel.

Later Mark with Jin will text for time to return and meet at college gate.

Undoubtedly couple arrive at college gate in taxi. Together cross busy street, turn left to walk down Long Mian West Road sidewalk. Dream-like adventure is in walking together among Tongcheng small shops, e-bikes parking on sidewalk and even students shopping and nodding their recognitions in twenty minute walk.

"Trip was long yesterday from Bundang, and rest is helpful but now feel fine," Jin said.

"Can we go eat in a restaurant?" Mark said.

"Yes. Heated and modern restaurant is up ahead on street nearby supermarket and share meals before with others," I said.

We walk into storefront on corner, climb up one flight of stairs to wall to wall windows and tables on second floor for midday Christmas meal. Restaurant is warm, comfortable to take off coats for meal.

"How is your beef steak Mark?" I said.

After meal we walk together few blocks away from restaurant for shopping at supermarket after our Christmas day lunch, and Mark shows Jin about store before taking escalator to third floor.

Touring many aisles on third floor, and passing shelves with choice of noodles Mark said, "Ooh, I am surprised. Dry noodles are more expensive in China than in South Korea."

We walk through upper level and look at bakery items and very large stuffed steamed buns. Couple buys a few things for their hotel room, and we depart shopping centre.

In pouring rain and darkness as shops are shutting down, we walk back to college campus to apartment on college campus. View from air-conditioned and heated bedroom window looks at parking lot for administrative offices filled with black cars between two buildings next to mountain. Bedroom curtains are open slightly or even wider in daytime to see views of Tongcheng mountain. Visiting with oldest son and wife, in this bedroom 25 December 2016, is location for one wall- heater in apartment for cold December winter night opening gifts together.

Walking to bedroom window to close curtains Mark said, "None of these Chinese people live like this. They all go home and live in luxury."

So then leave window curtains closed. Back at apartment David phones in afternoon as we are opening gifts to request attending celebration supper for Christmas Day.

"Mark please speak to David," I said.

Mark agrees and taking cellphone Mark said, "Thank-you. We have not seen each other in a long time so we choose to spend Christmas together and next day is fine."

Next day Boxing Day 26th December 2016, enjoy cooking eggs and bread gifts from supermarket before couple's arrival at apartment. We plan to go on tour of Old City, tourist suggestion from Maggie. Early in December Mark sends message to visit in Tongcheng, an arrival date in their short four day annual holiday and wish for us to visit local tourist sites. Maggie visits the apartment in late afternoon in early December 2016, with schedule for make-up class times before family visit and opens discussion of interest in English collocations.

Maggie said, "Mark can stay at same hotel for twenty-three yuan," and holds up two fingers and three fingers.

"What are suggestions for son's visit, and view tourist sites in Tongcheng and across street from college," I said.

"Old City," Maggie said.

"What is Old City," I said.

"Taxi driver will know if say Old City," Maggie said.

Mark and Jin agree to take Maggie's suggestion to tour Old City. Mark arrives early at apartment in morning next day 26th December, as Jin waits in taxi. Mark directs taxi driver to Old City, and discover trip will be close to one hour.

We proceed with trip down freeway out of Tongcheng, but to driver at Old City Mark said, "Can you return to meet later?"

"No. Ask at office in Old City," taxi driver said in English.

Cobble stone path down single lane at Old City is in clear weather and pass signs on posts outside of ancient buildings. School house is a large formal home-like building with offices on either side after entering. Small exterior hut in front is teacher lodgings with concrete slabs in teachers lodging.

Mark said, "At back looks like area of yard or water for bathing or drinking,"

We spend more time in this spot, of ancient school- times. Out in lane an accountant's office appears with signage.

Mark said, "Accounts for students are to be paid at this office Mom."

We wander to end of lane with large restaurant or club house appearing, and the pond is quiet and calm to stand for a few moments. As we all are enjoying our visit, we return back same lane to pass by military building.

I said, "Soldiers may have been here during revolution or war."

We continue on down narrow lane walking on large cobble bolders, and Mark said, "How about trying out tea house."

Tea house is quiet. As we are sitting, "How much is tea?" Mark said.

"Eighty yuan," server said.

Mark said, "Too much. Let's leave."

We wander farther on to business office, where future planning maps are on table with miniature gardens display. Mark arranges for our taxi, and manager walks with us out to parking lot with taxi soon arriving.

We take taxi back to Tongcheng and arrive at restaurant to meet David for Christmas celebration faculty supper on December 26. Opera students are attending meal and begin performing song sequences in traditional stage clothestands. Jin sitting on Mark's right, standing, begins recording students' drama and singing on her cellphone.

David sits to my left but speaking to Mark on right said, "Do you have any brothers or sisters?"

Mark said, "I am one of four sons."

David said, "Where are you staying?"

Mark said, "Jin reserves room before arrival in Tongcheng."

"Best hotel in Tongcheng," David said.

Mark said, "We are interested to visit local sites. Do you have suggestions."

Maggie said, "Visit museum of local famous opera singer next to Confucian Temple in City Square."

We leave supper together with Maggie and together cross Long Mian West Road to college gate. As I walk with Maggie in heavy rain, look over left shoulder and forever will see the imprint of oldest son, Mark, and wife Jin holding hands, walking behind us in lighted crosswalk in darkness of evening in rainy December in Tongcheng, China, my imagined dream.

Mark and Jin walk me to apartment from gate and return back to gate for taxi to hotel.

Later next day thank couple for attending faculty Christmas supper.

Mark said, "We had really good time."

After arriving from South Korea in December 2016, oldest son, Mark, helps for more comfort in apartment with purchases from nearby department store we pass on our walk to supermarket together. Mark and Jin buy blue basin for washing dishes in kitchen sink, soup ladle and kitchen things, blue clothes hangers and glass mug we choose for preparing green tea. They ask to return to department store to choose electric heating fan from group of fans on display inside front door, and choose orange color.

One morning Mark walks into dining apartment and said, "Jin thinks I need this black and white checkered chair cushion for one dining chair but I do not think so," and places cushion on chair.

Next evening Mark is assembling aluminum chest high clothes drying rack in apartment kitchen, cleaning stainless-steel kitchen sink for me and placing new blue basin purchase. We shop together and return to same department store for more purchases, even bar hand soap and powder laundry soap. Jin chooses new smaller thermos for hot water or tea for in my classes ten minute class break in back to back forty-five minute classes. Liquid laundry soap from overseas is making-do for hand-washing clothes in shower and hang-dry in heated bedroom. Mark visits in warmth of heated bedroom one evening as Jin calls to teach how to use washing machine.

Jin said, "Keep pushing buttons."

Following October 2017, department store is closing- down with street sales.

On the other hand from conversational English as foreign language classroom, view of college's main gate and large gold three-foot-high, shiny, brass Chinese letters outside are on classroom's window ledge. As we three walk up main road after passing through college gate, point out classroom to right in large academic building's second floor.

"Mark, look up there to large brass Chinese letters. Behind letters is classroom for English as foreign language classes," I said.

To Jin walking to our right, "There's Mom's classroom up there Jin!" Mark said.

We all glance at this multi-storey academic building. Jin turns to look at Chinese letters, then to us and smiles. Their hotel is within short taxi drive to college taking them past restaurant where coffee is bought as their taxi waits.

Mark said, "Hotel bed is hard and sleep is bad, breakfast food and cleanliness are very good and each day staff leave fresh basket of fruit and clean slippers."

Walking down Long Mian West Road from college to Tongcheng City Square in morning, we cross very busy intersection from supermarket and local bank, where do all banking, to visit historic site of National Museum of opera star. Construction and repairs to ten foot wall surround Confucian Temple. After crossing busy Square intersection we walk through front entrance to sign guest book at entrance with guardhouse. Many bus tours of Chinese tourists stop in front of temple to visit national landmark. Garden around quiet pond and an arch bridge in centre welcomes visitors. Inside temple nine gigantic twenty foot high statues sit in chairs in semi-circle. Outside I take my oldest son's photograph on cell phone on peaceful bridge inside temple walls. Jin heads first into museum with displays and photographs of local opera singer famous for national *Huangmei* opera, called Tea Picking Opera. Opposite temple courtyard, a military museum houses framed calligraphy Mark and I tour.

We chat about translations and suggest we tour Six Foot Alley. Entrance is across street from museum so pass through off main street walking down foot path and apartments on either side before lane will narrow to high walls in ivy on either side.

As we walk behind Jin is screaming. Mark runs up to Jin, chatting and hugging and returning to walk together said, "Jin is fine. Enjoying walk but looks up to see dead chicken hanging from window."

Once I return to sign guest book again March 2017, three months after my oldest son's visit, on warmer Festival March day-off from teaching conversational English.

Furthermore morning of our good-bye, son and wife invite me to walk together turning right out of college gate, walking lengthy block in separate pathway from Long Mian West Road past new building construction and vegetable gardens growing in abandoned lots to corner to street lights and crosswalks. They will return to hotel for packing up and taxi for one hour drive to Hefei fast train station for fast train to Shanghai. We stand in front of outdoor vegetable stands with fresh meat vendor's stand in background. Chatting on our last morning together in Christmas visit, as Jin stands nearby, Mark pulls out wallet to offer many Renminbi cash dollars to help pay for summer trip to Beijing.

Mark said, "Jin's parents in South Korea regret joining in their visit to China with them due to health issues and give them this financial gift to travel to China but it is more than spent in Tongcheng. We together decide and wish to help in my upcoming summer journey to study in Beijing."

MARKETS

In autumn after arriving in Tongcheng, find vegetable market and fruit shop ten minute walk from college to shop for home-cooking meals weekends and in winter vacations from January to February when canteen closes. Right turn from front gate down walkway separate from street traffic on busy Longmian West Road, tables sit outdoors under canopy with local vegetable vendors. Nearby indoor fruit market sells variety of fruits with tables outside advertising fruit prices. Outdoor vendor sells broccoli, local cabbage, greens, and potatoes and few packages of fried tofu. BBQ goose is sold at stand by same man each day riding his bicycle pulling a cart like a wagon with glass walls to show BBQ goose. Facing street mature stout lady sells every variety of tofu from various shapes in fried tofu and cutting off chunk from block to sell in small plastic bags. Always beside BBQ goose is cart to sell tofu near BBQ goose wagon.

Treats to me, varieties of fried tofu in squares and strips and large chunks of fresh tofu are among my choices to speak to portly lady tofu vendor about her brown tofu who said, "Fried."

Fresh tofu she is cutting into large rectangular blocks she measures and puts into small plastic bags or is counting her thin brown fried tofu into strips two centimetres by four centimetres. Home-cooking success is fried tofu with rice, broccoli, greens or Chinese cabbage from vegetable vendor and so cooking on electric hot plate with wok is in tranquil mountain view out my dining-room window on small square table. Squirrels roam and climb trees in view as steaming rice in rice-cooker sitting on floor near small cupboard on wheels with dishes to serve my food.

College is providing all cooking pans-like-new in boxes Maggie texts and said, "Walk across the parking lot outside apartment to go to speak to Dean of Maintenance nearby."

Dean of Maintenance is expecting visitor, foreign teacher, and checks boxes with new pots and pans before handing over. Mugs for tea are left behind already on kitchen counter.

Though in January 2018, learn new location of street vegetable and tofu vendors from Sue, during our work together on Saturdays at local business. Sue, who lives in house close to college with her child and mother, and she shares with another colleague, shops frequently at this market. David mentions shopping here too.

New location for vegetable street vendors "is close to old location but just off main street in lane," Sue said.

Extra work with Sue begins in second January 2018, from new relationship between college and local Tongcheng manufacturing company on Saturdays with Sue, college's business English colleague. After working at SinBon on Saturday, Sue and I are invited to share supper at large hotel with management.

Sue said, "In China, we do not waste any food, a difference from Western countries. We grow too much bamboo."

I said, "I love to see bamboo growing."

As I walk down busy Long Mian West Road, turn left and walk down narrow lane towards outdoor market, same vegetable stand's familiar clerk looks up and smiling greets me in camouflage hat with country's flag pin, returning from my last visit in June six months earlier. Broccoli, greens and potatoes are again short walk from second apartment to purchase for home-cooking meals.

In first two months winter holiday in January and February, while shopping at outdoor vegetable and fruit market, young woman begins speaking English to me and said, "What are you doing in Tongcheng!? How can you live here?"

I said, "I am Tongcheng College's English as foreign language teacher!"

"Cost of bananas is too much," young woman said and "husband negotiates with store's manager." She speaks English to explain family travels by train from Beijing to visit Tongcheng, her hometown and said, "Where are you living?"

I said, "I live in college's apartment on college campus."

She said, "Is kitchen an open air traditional Chinese kitchen?"

I said, "The kitchen is open air from sliding windows."

Friendly visitor to Tongcheng smiling said, "I even have difficulty speaking local dialect to speak with local Tongcheng citizens and Tongcheng is my hometown," as we stand together.

"Shopping is helped by store clerks with hand-motions as we agree on cost in amount on cash registers. English as foreign language classes are all spoken English for students learning conversational English," I said.

Undoubtedly returning to Tongcheng in October 2017, while shopping to buy yams at supermarket another male shopper at vegetable weighing-stand in produce section complains to clerk for foreigner to get in line properly. Clerk tells man to ignore foreigner as leave after this clerk weighs and bags produce and continue to check-out. Once as fresh tofu samples are on display at meat counter, woman shopper decides to help me choose tofu variety less spicy from selection of dishes of samples at meat counter I stop to try out. Her English is good and she mentions she is teacher in Tongcheng. She asks me about my activity so I explain I am foreign English teacher at nearby college. In my first year in Tongcheng, I buy fruit or vegetables at supermarket but also buy meat in my second-year contract. I walk past meat counter to find small packages of pork cutlets I purchase to cook my own pork meal with rice in second apartment.

Though while leaving supermarket on escalator to entrance from third floor, well-dressed man, on escalator behind me to my left, touches my shoulder to ask me in English said, "Are you teacher?"

I said, "Yes", and leave supermarket.

More than that in late February when sun is shining as leaving supermarket, young man asks me to go for ride on his large gasoline motorcycle. I shake my head to refuse, wave my hand to walk away to second apartment down busy street. In January 2018, in supermarket, find central table with small and large bags of imported oatmeal. Young female shopper is discussing purchase with her mother as I walk up to oatmeal display with excitement. Mother asks me about oatmeal with her smile and gesture holding up bag. I smile to hold bag closely indicating food is very good for breakfast. I purchase smaller bag and wish later for large bag because oatmeal is for sale again in expensive gift bags.

Nearby to college, small stores sell wide assortments of fruits choosing in second year. Once returning to second apartment in January holiday David, who is leaving his own apartment, asks to look in my bag, open my bag and to show him I have bought a lot of fruit at nearby market including Japanese plums and oranges. Fruit market across from college is new and easy to buy bananas most days.

Apples are costly in Tongcheng as even students mention in conversations in class said, "I do not know why apples cost so much in Tongcheng?"

Since rice warehouse sitting one half block down Long Mian West Road from college will sell large bag of twenty-five km rice, return with bag of rice to apartment.

At college meet female staff member before entering college gate who said, "How much do you pay?"

"Fifty yuan," I said.

No other comments are made. Often staff are able to purchase large quantity sizes of rice and cooking oil at canteen.

Even if supermarket entrance near City Square is through plastic hanging panels opening to main floor of small businesses, row of lockers for store shoppers' to store backpacks is at back of main floor before taking escalator in front of doorway to second floor. One security guard waits to evaluate new shoppers leaving second-floor escalator. Supermarket second-storey displays clothing, home supplies, pharmacy items and snack foods for sale. I buy toothpaste, during second year in Tongcheng, with help from two female clerks who call on younger male clerk who speaks some English. Varieties of toothpaste line shelf. Male clerk helps to advise me on toothpaste, and female clerk shows correct type of brand of toothpaste to purchase. Nearby on shelf also for sale are single packages of toothpick floss sticks. Female clerk suggests paying for items in pharmacy at cash register. During second winter vacation in 2018, try to buy barber scissors to cut hair. Help from college students unknown to me are shopping in supermarket and asking female supermarket clerk advice. Students find out no scissors are sold in supermarket from clerk.

Near wall past pharmacy department second escalator to third-floor moves past food displays to take shoppers up to large varieties of food items. Check out clerks stand in similar check-outs with cash registers and scales for weighing fruits and vegetables in front of wall of third floor. After I bag my items in my own shopping bags or sometimes with clerk's help, exit from supermarket is to right at end of wall to check-out clerks with sharp left turn where escalator takes shoppers down two-storeys to main entrance and where lockers are situated at back of main floor. Small receipts from row of selection of free lockers re-opens locker to pick up my backpack I can fill and carry my own bags full of purchases to walk down Long Mian West Road to college and my apartments both years.

HOLIDAY TIMES AND OPPORTUNITIES FOR LEISURE

Apartments are places of adventure to practise hobbies writing free verses, sketching, colouring and indoor photography. During first year in Tongcheng, supplies are from washing and drying used coffee paper filters for paper to draw local mountain with wax crayons. Resourcing material for drawing to afford supplies for sketching on reusable envelopes are efforts to learn to draw before arriving in Tongcheng. From small square table with window view colouring and drawing is beginning of reminders of lovely Tongcheng mountain. Daily, soon after arriving in Tongcheng, low treed mountain outside window is easy welcome after enjoying fresh filtered coffee from two bags of ground coffee. Son, Patrick, ships two packages of coffee, red plastic filter and paper filters to Post location in library and delivery to my apartment door in December 2016, and after returning to Seoul from their visit to Tongcheng, Mark ships coffee filters, ground coffee, socks and heating pads to stick to clothes to stay warm during classes in classrooms during cold winter weeks. Post delivery man brings packages from Mark to my apartment door in evening in late January.

Neither in October 2016, Joanna, student assistant, while walking together at playground and telling of upcoming rains prepares for results in time to avoid outdoor activity in rain such as daily three km walking schedules at playground. Subtropical rains are heavier, more violent than any rain. Walking in rain without umbrella back home is common in my country and continue to walk in rain in Tongcheng. After arriving in Tongcheng, locals arm-wave to stay out of these rains. Horrid results develop from exposure to rains with burning and peeling of reddened burnt facial skin and needing more rest from exhaustion.

After seeing skin damage in the classroom five year English Major student, Joyce, helping recovery with advice said in class and while walking to canteen, "Drink a lot of water, at least one litre daily, stay inside resting out of rains and indoors from twelve noon to two in afternoon breaks from classes as pollution is much worse from traffic at noon hour."

After first heavy rains pass and walking to Tongcheng Square on Saturday to go to Bank of China sophomore student, Santorini is advertising restaurant she works at on sidewalk with others and said, "What happens to your face?"

"Walking in heavy rains is causing condition of red, peeling skin," I said.

Santorini suggests sharing lunch. "Must walk to bank as need to withdraw cash," I said.

Santorini offers to pay for lunch where Santorini is waitress. Deli House restaurant is upstairs and follow Santorini through main floor shoe store to staircase. Second-story interior with windows and window English sign for Deli House faces a busy street corner and is above quiet coffee shop. Santorini chooses window table with view of large bakery on corner. Restaurant is busy and menu is Western style food. Santorini orders dishes to please and enjoy lunch together. Santorini said, "Santorini name describes beautiful location in Greece in photograph.

Deli House with Western style food is suggestion to son and wife during their four day vacation to China two months later in December. Restaurant is heated to enjoy sharing more than one meal together. Mark asks for Maggie's text number to surprise me and our last meal is at another heated restaurant we celebrate with menus of alcohol and Western or Chinese food and salad bar with deserts. Second restaurant we visit is in building with theatre and restaurants and elevator from street level on evening before their departure from Tongcheng. Their plans include a stopover in Shanghai for New Years celebrations before home to South Korea.

On other hand, after returning to Tongcheng in October 2017, Deli House restaurant closes. An empty space is on second floor from street level. One warm spring day later in February 2018, male stylists are on sidewalk and street with fireworks on the street curb to advertise as walk past as far away as possible on sidewalk from their drama. Nearby at busy four-way intersection, one policeman stands in winter on busy Saturdays, and in warmer spring weather when more cars drive through to city's Square. Policeman stands with whistle directing traffic in all types of weather and smog. Son, Patrick, suggests before arrive in Tongcheng to walk with flow of people and crowds and for this reason learn to wait for others to cross busy and noisy-streets with e-bikes and cars on walks to bank, mall markets or supermarket.

At Tongcheng College, the round boulevard with one huge rock in centre and painted letters leads uphill after passing through guarded main gate past large grassy lawns and tiled pathways to college's two main six-storey buildings and college library on left. Grasses in uncut lengths are picked by hand by college gardeners. To right after walking up sidewalk from round boulevard apartments on right are where I will live following year returning to Tongcheng College as foreign English teacher.

Months after arriving one evening walking together after staff meal in restaurant, and as she accompanies me home to my first apartment pass lighted windows of apartments. Maggie said, "Families enjoy home for many years in these apartments."

At top of hill main entrance doorway is on side facing downhill opposite rectangular row of darkened administrative offices belonging to maintenance and faculty on right. Maggie will walk together through doorway and very dark zigzag stairwell to fourth-floor until outside apartment doorway on covered balcony. Lights of library might be on or neighbors on corner arriving or departing.

Yet first year in Tongcheng in 2016, Maggie suggests sister's apartment after hiking and one occasion for lunch. Three of us sit together Sunday eating midday meal sister cooks before going to work. Her husband works in different city and Maggie's sister works in medical supply business they explain at our lunch.

"What business is your father in?" I said.

Maggie said, "Father works in business."

Maggie's sister's large apartment's front door, on upper floor of apartment building, opens from interior zigzag concrete staircase we enter and climb from back where parking is located for Maggie's e-bike. Modern bathroom, stairway leading from living room to master bedroom and two other bedrooms are on main floor. Kitchen is separate room where Maggie's sister cooks and is visible from dining room table where Maggie and I sit chatting and wait on our meal. We enjoy spare ribs family recipe Maggie's sister said, "Cook for guest."

In front of apartment building is office to receive mail order packages. Maggie's sister looks for her order as we leave her apartment together. Maggie explains to me year before she pays rent to sister for food to live in their apartment while her own apartment is being finished and returns to college from studying her masters degree. One visit, twin nieces ask to accompany me back to college on city bus as Maggie must leave earlier for appointment. Twin girls are young teenagers, thirteen years old and notice shoes for sale as we pass on our walk to bus stop they say are expensive. Generosity from girls is welcome to buy bus tickets to arrive at bus stop in front of college gate and depart to walk to apartment and girls will take another bus to return to their home.

Yet vegetables are photographic to learn names of these local foods. One day in late October 2016, as leave apartment for daily walk at playground on Saturday morning on left inside low wall view tree past weeks with fruit ripening to bright orange like peach tree fruit in my Western country. As walk past neighbour's home this Saturday morning greet male neighbour in Mandarin. Neighbour is up ladder in fruit tree in his apartment building courtyard in apartment block on left downhill leaving from apartment. After departing Tongcheng and returning in next ten-month contract year later, live above this same neighbour in three bedroom second apartment. Neighbour motions to bring bag to him on this Saturday morning. Abundant fruit growing in his tree for weeks looks like ripening peaches to mention in class with students and speak of as example of favourite fruit, a peach, for English conversation of favourite fruit. Small plastic green plaid bag in backpack found earlier during walk at playground fills with fruit from his tree. Photograph of one piece of tree fruit oldest son, Mark, in South Korea writes of explaining name of fruit as persimmon. In next days make persimmon soup out of fruit too.

Canteen staff are friendly in their eating place. Plastic philodendrons and plastic fruits circle above in fluorescent lighting in ceiling to enjoy meals and drinks for breakfast, lunch and supper. Breakfast meal choices are varieties of rice porridges, called congee, plain or green tea boiled eggs, fried dumplings, and steamed buns either filled with vegetables, meat or unfilled for breakfast, but also lunch or supper. Breakfast meal is my time to enjoy congee. Hot-cooked rice resembles oatmeal with splash of hot milk. Huge plates of steamed rice are added by server to plate to add one or two varieties from choices of tofu, green vegetables, duck, beef, pork and chicken for lunch and supper sold on both floors of large canteen. Breakfast or lunch tables are filled by hundreds of students and staff, and supper a quieter eating event. During my first welcome meal in autumn 2016, Headmaster Wu said, "Do you like canteen food?" "Food is exceptional to enjoy," I said. Favourite canteen meal becomes deep fried chicken with rice and warm soy milk selling from drink bar. Joanna first tells about delicious warm and soothing soy milk drink she enjoys as we share breakfast early before eight o'clock morning classes. Drink bar added on canteen's second floor in second year sells ice cream, coffee and cold drinks.

After returning second year to college, decide to increase quantity of food to eat for meals. One Renminbi buys plain boiled egg and added to two hot steamed buns, with or without vegetables and once in awhile dumplings for before classes and weekends.

However, "Free vats of liquid seaweed soup are on second floor," Joanna said, "for freshman."

And learn anyone is welcome to add to their meal liquid soup by taking small metal bowl from stack and metal spoon from tray. Very large groups of students surround large stainless steal soup pots to take turns dishing soup. Often students may help to serve me before serving their own soup at this small table at front of canteen at large dark red tile pillar.

"One yuan is deducted from cost of each meal on second floor of canteen," Maggie said after returning to Tongcheng.

Large lunch crowds common in front of canteen servers, so one lunchtime

English Corner colleague said, "Teachers go behind counter to servers' stations to be served first."

Canteen server sees foreign teacher appear, heaping extra rice onto plate before we choose food from wide selection. Once in awhile senior students join me for lunch from our small five-year English Major classes.

On one occasion for lunch, President Shen stops by my table during lunch to look at my meal said, "It is tofu?"

Arriving in Tongcheng Maggie explains advantages of clean air quality near local mountain. During winter holiday times, in my apartment rest, stay in touch with family by internet, practice hobby of illustrating local mountain with crayon onto reusable paper coffee filters, or get daily exercise and complete ten km walking at playground. Free time at same small square table, my resource during both winter holidays, illustrate local mountain nearby many college buildings, either in view from windows in front of me as in first apartment or from memory in wax crayon from playground. as in first apartment or from memory in wax crayon from playground.

At end of our third term December 2017, at students' performances in auditorium Maggie said, "Winter holiday is lasting from January until first week of March and longer winter vacation. What are internet pages for improving English skills?"

I said, "WordPress is fine in China."

Year before Headmaster Wu and faculty arrange visit to neighbouring city, Anqing at end of first term in late December 2016, after son's visit with wife to Tongcheng. At our second celebration meal, hosted by Headmaster Wu sitting to my right, Maggie is sitting to my left and senior college administrators sit around table in dining-room on second floor of nearby restaurant to college. Their local guest, who is leaving Tongcheng to study his PhD, joins us. Arriving early with Maggie speak with senior Administrator waiting, and after returning to college Administrator will become next year's apartment building neighbour.

Furthermore, Maggie meets early next Saturday morning and asks to join to visit small corner restaurant across from college gate for warm soymilk while we wait to travel one hour in black college sedan to Anqing. In October we apply together with colleagues for Permanent Resident Permit in Anqing. President Shen, of college, is meeting us at college gate to celebrate gift and seeing us off in black college sedan is waving and smiling.

In Anqing, we are driven to salmon-coloured gated stucco apartment complex to join and meet Headmaster Wu's wife, Hong Wei Wu, primary school teacher Maggie is explaining in car. Hong meets us outside her apartment's gate to sit in front seat. We will continue to drive in college sedan to location to tour local and famous royal blue Buddhist Temple across street from Yangtze River and visit downtown mall where Headmaster Wu requests at our faculty supper we are to have ice cream.

Moreover in arrival in front entrance of temple Headmaster Wu's wife, Hong said, "freedom of religion is allowed and I am a Christian."

Indeed cushions and baskets on floor nearby, where we three stand together left unsupervised, visitors come and go to kneel at Anqing Buddhist Temple. Traditional monks walk from their apartment doors and to rooms inside courtyard and front entrance to temple. Temple's steeple is like thick needle about two people widths protruding into sky with staircase that wraps around outside entire height of steeple. Maggie asks to climb winding steep staircase with her to top of steeple. Maggie laughs a lot as follow to climb narrow winding stairs as others also climb.

Hong is choosing to wait, as she said, "No. Climbing is foolish."

Maggie helps Hong with translations in our conversations.

At top of temple steeple, a breathtaking view emerges of great Yangtze River flowing north and south with river's two-storey river ferries sailing in two directions. As we leave courtyard below, outside wide flat, waste-high shelves like tables fill with burning incense one or two visitors light in sunny weather.

Aromas from burning incense carries us down stairs and outside where scanty couple street beggars sit, and stairs leads us outside temple with briskly flowing Yangtze River across road to hail taxi to city mall. Maggie follows Headmaster Wu's instructions so first thing; Maggie treats us at centre mall stand to enjoy ice cream seated together before touring mall and stopping for lunch at mall restaurant.

Another foreign teacher, a woman using a walker, sees us seated outside restaurant waiting for vacant seats and walks towards us to ask said, "Are you a foreign teacher?"

We stand to speak to her and Hong, on my left, tells foreign teacher she has taken her English speaking course at local church where Anqing foreign teacher volunteers.

Woman said, "I am from Pennsylvania and come to Anqing twenty-five years ago. I think this is my last year. I went to USA recently for visit home."

Waiting with her Chinese colleague, foreign teacher asks about me as we all wait in crowd to be seated in restaurant.

"My home is in Canada," I said.

Foreign teacher is surprised at number of classes I teach, as eighteen, comparing these to her ten classes each week half her number of classes.

Soon sitting inside restaurant, American sits with one Chinese colleague at nearby tables. During lunch, offer Hong flag pin from my home country and Hong leaves and returns in ten minutes with lovely shawl gift she purchases. Outside mall where we wait on taxi, a very large Christmas tree stands decorated.

Hong said, "Anqing is growing quickly from new chemical plant industry and we stand in area of new growth. Anqing is rich with culture."

In our taxi together to Tongcheng, Hong sits in front seat, asks for email and text information. Headmaster Wu maintains separate second apartment near college due to demanding schedules and later discover Hong's hometown is Tongcheng where her mother continues to reside.

Waste high cedar hedge carving of Chinese letters across twenty foot length hedge and visible as walk down main avenue from playground and to or from canteen to apartments both years is background in courtyard with large sculpture in grey stone leading to music school. To enter apartment after returning to Tongcheng and until July 2018, walk by this hedge daily across music school's courtyard to next building. In final weeks, stop nearby hedge to take few cellphone photographs. Closer look of sculpture seems to be large dolphin but with row of shark-like teeth. Small park sits between main college avenue, music school courtyard and hedge. Walking on pebbled path through gentle low hedges and small trees to foreign teachers new and second apartment celebrates extraordinary return to Tongcheng to work at college teaching English as foreign language in conversational English.

Though, after arriving in China and first trip to Tongcheng from fast train station in Hefei in college's black sedan with hired driver, David's invitation to share lunch is in bright casual restaurant where experience first public bathroom with no toilet paper and at floor level. Maggie offers me tissue. At lunch, Maggie mentions my university as in top ten from my country. After leaving restaurant in same taxi, as driver joins our lunch, and Maggie completes hotel registration at hotel across street from college, male colleague on street outside hotel said, "Foreigner must report to local police station within twenty-four hours after arriving in Tongcheng." We depart to walk to local police station with passport to speak to local Tongcheng police officer. We are both told to wait in police officer's office. In chairs opposite plain clothes officer with Maggie on right, male police officer speaks Chinese to Maggie as he reviews foreign passport with Z Visa issued from Chinese Visa Centre in home country. Meeting takes less than fifteen minutes and we leave to attend celebration dinner near hotel staying in across street from college, and change to clean T-shirt, a sparkly print, for special occasion many college staff attend.

Since canteen closes during both college, two-month winter holidays indulging and enjoy breakfast at street vendor locations with great tasting green-tea boiled eggs and very large stuffed steamed buns. Vendor sets up shop with his big pots and grill in small opening next to bakery and corner convenience store. Most locals are passing by or stand in line behind but this vendor always helps me choose choice of stuffed, extra large steamed buns. His green tea boiled eggs are enjoyable, sometimes cracked, but much less expensive than canteen green tea boiled eggs for this adventure to Tongcheng with local Tongcheng folks. Next door bakery on corner serves fried steamed buns on large flat grill outdoors each morning, delicious and appealing often stopping for. Maggie bought my first fried white steamed bun I am stunned at how delicious as Maggie complains they are very good but stops often and quits buying. Couple with child and parents operate small street bakery and cook at site. Fried white steamed buns sit outside on warming pan similar to large Western- style grill. Second large white loaf with lovely fruit stamp for luxury purchase from this bakery second year celebrates Spring Festival. David gives me first loaf of this delectable seasonal festive heavy white bread few weeks before and decide to buy second loaf too.

Meanwhile after arriving in Tongcheng, Maggie often is asking to go hiking on Sundays to countryside and mountain location of countryside Buddhist Temple, twenty minute e-bike ride from college. Once local police officer is hiking in my first spring and sharing greetings with Maggie. Outside gold-yellow low monk dwellings are simple benches and we sit.

Maggie said, "I visit temple on mountain alone and often am visiting with monk living at and caring for Buddhist Temple. Monk, who is kind too, and when she hikes by herself."

Monk is often seen near his small dwelling near temple working in building or enjoying sitting in sunshine on his small bench. Tall temple steeple, near monk's residence and workshop, welcomes visitors in steps to circular balcony, an opening to interior and stairs to climb inside temple up inside steeple. Visitors wander around on temple exterior balcony to witness vast east and west views of valley leading to Tongcheng or away to countryside. Maggie explains monks live in isolation on mountain and often locals in past bring food to monks living on mountain unable to depart home of temple. Midway on winding mountain road to temple, new temple is in construction soon to open near large complex of residences.

After hiking with Maggie couple times we go to friend's home to help tutor their daughter. Maggie tapes my voice reading script to be used later as example of native speaker. Family owns small hotel and home is above hotel. Middle-school age student is upstairs in her room in tight spaces and her mother gives me some baking as we depart and works behind hotel desk as gratitude. One time, we are both invited to join family for hot pot dinner Sunday evening in restaurant near movie theatre in same building and floor as restaurant of farewell dinner with Mark and Jin evening before their departure back to Seoul weeks earlier. Restaurant is in large building near Tongcheng Square. We sit at booth with inset large pot. Then mother invites us to choose food to cook at restaurant buffet. Food is brought to table and we cook our meals together.

On other hand weeks later in spring ride on Maggie's pink e-bike to riverside near Tongcheng to hike and view hydro water installation for Tongcheng. Maggie parks her e-bike on side of road and we walk up wide pathway to view large concrete dam and building for hydro power plant in distance across local river.

Maggie joking with me about concrete barrier for dam we stand above said, "I walk all over concrete barrier by myself before."

At riverside on our return to Maggie's e-bike sitting parked on side of road, man beats clothes with his washing stick in river and in road in front of homes, washed laundry hangs on sunny spring day.

Nevertheless in June 2017, casual meeting with Maggie evolving in canteen on warm morning as sit near open doors and eating congee for breakfast in views of trees and student dormitories.

Maggie is sitting across from me and explains to me Anqing Bureau of Exits and Entrances police officer said, "Bureau will renew Maureen's Z Visa to remain in Tongcheng."

Maggie said, "You will not be returning to Tongcheng."

We leave canteen together and Maggie walking beside said, "You must get different Visa to stay in China to go to Beijing."

Second year contract with employer is signed with Lynn of Echo Education in Hangzhou in January 2017, to return to China for second ten-month contract and Lynn advising to return to Tongcheng.

I said, "Yes, I will travel to Hong Kong to apply for new Visa to attend training in Beijing."

Oldest son, Mark, comment after visiting me in Tongcheng December 2016, is in shock I will return as he said, "Tongcheng is remote area in boondocks."

Though Maggie calls me by video welcoming me to Tongcheng before leaving home country for Tongcheng in October 2017, as we continue relationship and our work in English as foreign language for young adults in conversational English classes.

ADAPTING TO FESTIVALS, HOLIDAYS AND SPECIAL SPECIFIC DAYS

"Mooncake Festival" also called "Mid-Autumn Festival"

Weeks after first of two arrivals in Tongcheng, Maggie texts to join her and sister to drive to countryside to their family home for Mid-Autumn Festival celebration. David is suggesting outing to Maggie. Earlier in week friendly female Hotel Major student describes Mooncake Festival to me in classroom, and gives me moon cake, a delicious treat, as we pass by each other walking to and from classes and canteen.

On drive to their parents' family home in countryside with her sister driving, Maggie said, "Do farm homes in your country resemble country homes we are driving past?"

I said, "Farm homes in my country are simpler, smaller."

Driving past large, peaceful pond in our arrival, Maggie is telling pond is shared by her father and uncle for fishing and they hire guards to prevent poaching and outsiders from fishing pond. In next spring while together on Sunday to go hiking on local Buddhist mountain Maggie explains, so I understand more, in winter everyone is gathering around wood stove to stay warm in homes without central heating. Maggie's sister parks her black sedan in front of purple formal doorway and entrance to interior open air courtyard of parents' home and later send information in emails to family

Doorways open from home's interior courtyard to kitchen, dining room, and bedrooms nearby. Maggie's father is peeling garlic cloves from large basket of garlic and is sitting on back doorstep leading out courtyard's rear doorway looking onto large pond, country road and tranquil countryside.

Maggie standing beside me near her father said, "In China we call land where vegetables grow fields but where you live vegetables grow in gardens."

Maggie's mother washes her underwear and hangs up her washing in sunny open-air courtyard. Standing alone in courtyard for brief minutes nearby cupboard son-in-law is counting chopsticks, and assists with table setting in formal dining room with doorway from courtyard. Maggie is giving tour of her parents home. Maggie's bedroom, with tidy double bed is adorned with many pink cushions. We walk to kitchen where large stove like wood stove holds many dishes in large pots and mother and daughters cook. Through kitchen window is view of backyard bird pen and ducks stroll about. Maggie said, "Doorway is across kitchen to bathroom." Maggie is youngest of four daughters.

Indeed Maggie invites me into dining room where Maggie sits on my right and Maggie's mother and father to my left. Many dishes are served in meal Maggie's mother and sisters prepare since morning. Dishes of vegetables, duck, pig, and fish sit in middle of large dining table. Maggie tells names of each food in dishes as dish is passed to me. I look up to my left to see large portrait of Chairman Mao in centre of wall. Gift of book from oldest son from South Korea reminds me of story of young man, Mao Zedong, who lives in China's countryside where Communist revolution begins. Sister's video call with her husband starts with Maggie's sister sitting across our table and her husband in Ipad-like video welcomes me and shows husband's father in hospital bed in hospital.

Maggie said, "Say hello to sister's father-in-law in hospital bed."

I said, "Hello *Ni hao,"* and in Mandarin to sister's father-in-law smiling seeming to enjoy.

To left of Chairman Mao's portrait, in corner of separate dining room and behind my chair, large stainless steel container sits with two large stacked doors. I said, "Maggie," sitting on my right, "is this a refrigerator?"

"Yes, container is refrigerator," Maggie said.

In that moment ask Maggie for advice with my college apartment to move stainless steel refrigerator from kitchen to dining room area. Maggie agrees to help next week. After meal is over, Maggie's sister and twin daughters, and Maggie say goodbyes.

I said to Maggie's mother for invitation to festival in Mandarin, "*Shi shi.*"

Outside sister's black car sits in driveway and we all get into car. Sisters' uncle passes by car to speak to them and Maggie's sister, twin daughters and Maggie speak in happy unison to their uncle, their father's brother Maggie shares. Maggie is taking driving lessons and does not require licence to drive e-bike Maggie tells me in car. We drive for one hour back to college campus where Maggie's sister drives through college gate back to my apartment with friendly goodbyes.

CHINESE NEW YEAR'S AND SPRING FESTIVAL

Afternoon is quiet and security guards are located across parking lot outside first apartment at row of administration offices as I stand waiting. Maggie rides up on her pink e-bike to transport me to family's New Year's celebration at her own apartment. I visit Maggie's apartment times during our Sunday hiking excursions. Male student describes, in English conversation classes confirming with students, Spring Festival is favourite festival when families visit in afternoons to share plates of dumplings together. After returning to college next October and eating supper in canteen, freshman students invite me in canteen to assist to make dumplings as activity. Students sit across and beside me as we are brought trays of cut dough pieces and fillings from canteen for dumplings to our long table with freshman students by canteen staff. Students teach me methods and making styles of dumplings as dumplings vary with region with fold overs or pressing sides of dumplings with fillings as we sit together at long table on second floor of canteen.

In Maggie's apartment in January, I meet family members from Mooncake Festival months earlier at Maggie's parents' home in countryside in October and now also meet Maggie's paternal grandfather. Earlier Maggie tells me she is purchasing apartment when apartment is being built with only concrete walls so is choosing all finishing. Her mother is telling me there are neighbours above apartment as she points up. I bring flag pins from my native country to share as gifts, offer four pins to Maggie's mother, and sit them on dining table. Maggie shows me through apartment and greet her twin nieces stretching out on Maggie's double bed.

Maggie's apartment is new with two bedrooms, one modern bathroom, compact kitchen with sliding doors to dining area and large living room opens to enclosed balcony then am invited to sit on white ornate sofa opposite television set as Maggie said, "This is grandfather."

Smog is thick New Year's day 27 January 2017, looking out through sliding glass patio doors to enclosed balcony of Maggie's apartment on twenty-sixth floor to other apartment high rises standing in smog. Comedy show is airing from China and starring Western Chinese movie star Jackie Chan in live performance in entertainment competition. Grandfather sits quietly on my left with his son, Maggie's father, who comes to sit beside him. Grandfather tries to nod and we sit and enjoy television. Sunflower seeds are holiday treat in bowl on white coffee table. Maggie comes to sit on my left by my side on sofa to speak English to grandfather, and father sits on matching love seat to our left.

I said, "Maggie, how much time do sister and mother work to prepare traditional meal of mutton and beef and vegetables?"

"They work entire day from morning," Maggie said.

As we all are seated at Maggie's dining table in combination living-dining room, Maggie's father tells me to eat a lot of meat and I eat as much as possible. Arguments begin at meal between Maggie's father and Maggie, who sits on my right texting entire meal. Maggie's father is sitting at end of table on my left. Later, at ten pm, we return on Maggie's e-bike back to my first apartment. Maggie apologizes for family disagreement and regrets my experience. On e-bike ride through streets of stores, restaurants and homes with fireworks lighted nearby by young men running in streets, sky ignites with bangs from exploding fireworks sparkling in every direction lighting up sky. Fireworks continue for twenty-four hours. Youngest son, Justin, visit by internet video chat very next day and explain fireworks noises going on all night and New Year's celebration with loud explosions of fireworks continuing into the new day.

In addition walking across street from college to cellphone store with same name as Hangzhou store and college store is to pay account. Small store is run as family business with grandparents, daughter and child in small store. Daughter makes phone call when she sees me and Dean of English's assistant, Mr. Ye, comes to store and mentions he is out shopping.

He is shocked I am in Tongcheng for holiday and so gives me packaged tofu and congee from his shopping bag and said, "How do you survive? What do you eat? Canteen is closed."

Mr. Ye helps me to pay account and explains cellphone store clerk suggests to open different account which will cost much less for five months to text and calls limited to college campus until June departure. Later I ask Maggie to help to change account and said, "Did you walk across street with Mr. Ye?" New paper work is drawn up with store Maggie helps translate.

At cellphone store, Mr. Ye invites me to Mr. Ye's wife's parents' family home for New Year's holiday meal but first Mr. Ye said, "Do you have any more pins from your country?"

"Yes, I have many pins" I said.

Mr. Ye and I walk across street through college gate and uphill to my apartment where inside retrieve four official flag pins as he waits outside. We walk back across street to walk blocks to his large apartment near college. As we enter apartment Mr. Ye explains son may decide to travel overseas to continue education. His son inside apartment, studying, is given pin from me, introduces me and then Mr. Ye gives me fruit, an apple. Mr. Ye's small car is parked outside in parking lot. I went with Mr. Ye to small garage where his car oil is changed a short distance off main street.

I sit on chair to watch. Nearby garage, home keeps rooster and chickens in small yard. During our drive together Mr. Ye tells me previous English as foreign language teacher marries local girl, have one child but teacher, wife and child rent apartment off campus nearby as couple's relationship offends students. Foreign teacher drinks liquor with his mother-in-law as payment for mother-in-law teaching foreign teacher Mandarin. Foreign teacher stays three years in Tongcheng.

In our car ride Mr. Ye said, "Foreign teacher goes to Hong Kong for Visa and wife and their child stay in Tongcheng. Costs for obtaining a driver's licence are high."

Mr. Ye drives to his wife's family's apartment, and where Mr. Ye is sharing news of the foreign teacher, who is alone for lengthy holiday for New Year's celebration. Family members arrive including two sisters of assistant administrator's wife. One younger sister-in-law is asked by Mr. Ye if she works in bank. A large round table topper is propped against dining-room wall and brought from wall to be placed over top of smaller round table. At dining table, I give out another two pins to father-in-law, sitting on my left, and Mr. Ye sits on my right. Father-in-law invites me to share drink of clear high proof alcohol in similar small glasses others are using I decline. Meal is passed in chatter and soon family leave table for large room to play cards. Roomy apartment is very cold, unheated and no one takes off their coat in cold apartment. Enclosed kitchen is to right of front doorway and enclosed balcony to left of living-room. Second sister and husband are at card table.

As I am invited to sit on sofa, younger sister invites me to watch said, "Do you enjoy English TV Channel?"

"Yes," I said, as she adjusts television to watch English channel for another three hours in midst former astronaut interviews while visiting Beijing for his experience in space with family card games in large next room.

In fact going out to walk at playground both years on New Year's Days is on quiet campus where locals may be visiting as students are absent for vacation in hometowns. After returning to Tongcheng for second contract, fireworks prohibition is in effect after midnight and view fireworks in local park at midnight from second apartment's bedroom window or hear and see fireworks from second apartment's kitchen window to north at playground.

TOMB SWEEPING FESTIVAL KNOWN AS *QINGMING* FESTIVAL

During March Tomb Sweeping Festival national holiday, families visit Tongcheng's mountain to visit their family tombs, smoothly-shaped grey concrete enclosures about four feet high and six to eight feet long to put flowers at small doors of tomb or near family tomb and light fireworks and sparklers. Mountain is decorated over eastern side, near playground, with colourful flowers and decorations. One time in springtime 2017, as I return to first apartment from playground, three people plant fireworks over centre face of mountain above administration parking lot among trees resembling past orchard of apple or plum trees with white blossoms in spring. Two young men and one young woman climb front of Tongcheng mountain near first apartment igniting fireworks. On left front west side of mountain another family arrives planting and lighting fireworks in afternoon on warm March Sunday I witness from open kitchen windows. Most celebrations take place on Sunday of Tomb Sweeping Festival. After returning to Tongcheng and second Tomb Sweeping Festival, I write description of festival to my second oldest son, Patrick, who shares his joy and admiration.

More than that first description of Tomb Sweeping Festival is from Headmaster Wu in hallway outside English as foreign language classroom after he and Maggie visit class of over forty freshman students in English Major program in early March 2017. Maggie sends text message shortly before class I describe to classroom of nervous students I advise to stay calm to enjoy visit. Headmaster Wu and Maggie sit at back of class for two forty-five minute English as foreign language lessons to hear lesson plans I design. After lively classroom lesson of debate between two teams of students standing on either side of classroom,

Maggie walks up to foreign teacher's desk on raised platform in front of large class of more than forty students, and leaning over said, "Your classroom content is adequate with lesson plan to teach speaking opinions in English in debate, hearing poetry spoken from my own small book of poetry, and reading paragraphs from simplified version from Wishbone Classics of Shakespeare's Oliver Twist by Charles Dickens."

I bring books with me from abroad to China to use as lesson resources.

After this class, leave classroom to stand in hallway with Headmaster Wu and Maggie as we visit, and Headmaster Wu describes in his own English words upcoming important *Qingming* Festival March 27 called Tomb Sweeping with many days off. Maggie translates Headmaster's spoken English explanation to me. Female colleague walks past us from office next door to classroom, and with who we try to smile as Headmaster Wu smiles also. Tomb Sweeping Festival is time off from regular classes for few days and canteen and stores close, like supermarket Headmaster Wu amplifies.

INTERNATIONAL WOMEN'S DAY

On an afternoon March 08, 2017, Maggie invites me to her office.

Maggie said to our group of students, "The day is International Women's Day in China."

I said, "Day is known as International Women's Day event for girls and women everywhere," to students in Maggie's office.

LABOR DAY, NATIONAL DAY AND CHILDREN'S DAY FESTIVALS

Students randomly remind me of special days in classrooms or walking together at playground and on campus. Labor Day in China, May 1, is traditional event called May Day in places and locations we discuss in English as foreign language conversations in class.

During our classes both years in spring in Tongcheng, students speak up in class, "June 1 is Children's Day Festival with special attention paid to small children from government and families for activities."

National Day, October 05, students said, "Honours founding of People's Republic of China."

Students speaking English to me even at canteen or walking to and from dormitories and two apartments for two years, describe or announce festivals. At beginnings or endings of our classes, in free-speaking I often ask for anyone to speak as long as descriptions are in English words on any topic or event.

DRAGON BOAT FESTIVAL

During shopping visits to supermarket, shoppers are stocking up on sticky rice dumplings, "*zongzi*," rice wrapped in bamboo. Hong is beginning her visits in first year in Tongcheng during May and month of this festival. Hong texts of writing children's poetry books and texts pictures of poetry books. Hong brings many food gifts both years in Tongcheng. Maggie is joining us to go out for tea and to walk down Long Mian West Road in hot weather. Hong is carrying her yellow umbrella but said, "I like to wear a hat so I can move my arms."

Eva, employer representative in Hangzhou, often is sending notes to foreign teachers at any destination in China. Eva's description of Dragon Boat Festival is helping to learn drama of festival is in story of ancient patriotic poet, Qu Yuan, in conflict with ancient local government using poet's poetry for legal effect on population. Poet's story is tragedy of suicide May 5 in Miluo River, branch of Yantze River, with large rock he ropes around himself for suicide to drown in river. Hong is bringing many gifts of bamboo wrapped sticky-rice and duck eggs. Duck eggs are given from me to Maggie to share. Hong brings wrapped square lovely sweet cookies in small clear packages produced in Anqing both these festivals we share in Tongcheng.

CHRISTMAS, EARTH DAY, FATHER'S DAY, MOTHER'S DAY, EASTER

Classroom is place to discuss in conversational English methods students use to celebrate and gift giving. Personal gifts may be in-person or messages are sent from students on their cellphones students describe in our classes and may be costly with texting gifts or simple messages. On these occasions discussions of types of cellphones evolve with students describing cell phone choices.

During conversation student said, “My cellphone is Huawei but very cheap phone.” Student goes on, “The maker is company run by woman and her father from military.”

Most important, on first Mother’s Day Sunday in Tongcheng, text from Joanna invites me to visit training school with her and student to share this day. We meet across from college to buy steamed buns and dumplings with another student, Nancy. Joanna and Nancy decide to hail taxi to attend training school’s Mother’s Day event, 14 May 2017. Crafting event, with training school students and staff from Bluniverse Training School, is held at craft and social club in newer building. Building’s guard sits on main floor of building students explain our visit to. Elevator takes us to higher floor where we gather in booths waiting for event. Later, we sit around large crafting table together with children from Bluniverse Training School and parents with children, either a father or mother asking questions to foreign teacher at same time discussing English expressions, with myself seated at head of table and Joanna on my left. Joanna and Nancy write email addresses into my Mother’s Day event card. Eric and Helen, Bluniverse teachers, also sign my card as teachers at this training school. Mothers and fathers of students sit with students as I walk around table to speak to each child. Few do speak to me with easy questions and listen to my presentation. I write poem into store bought card from Joanna, Nancy, Eric and Helen with four leaf clover on back from Red Rose Stationery Ltd. Pictures in card are in sparkles of stack of books, pencils and school bus van with butterflies in pink and blue flying. I read my poem to our group.

Today is Mother’s Day

Thank you for sharing

Warmth together

Is always

Being somewhere too. Maureen May 14, 2017.

Below my written poem, signatures from Eric, Joanna, Nancy and Helen are listed. Few students play games for male Bluniverse teacher as I stand nearby watching small presentations. Eric drives Joanna, Nancy and myself to return to college. In text to Maggie about event to let her know I attend without payment, Maggie texts is fine.

"Take Me To Your Heart" is song popular with students in large auditorium with student-led performances. Joanna, my student assistant, sings at student amateur shows, and students in crowded audiences shout their gratitude to Joanna singing this song in her pleasant voice with ability to reach higher notes.

"A Little Love" is second favourite with words, *Greatness as you, Smallest as me, You show me what is deep as sea, A little love, little kiss.....*

Joanna often is familiar and able to discuss holidays like Easter and as Christian speaking of Jesus in class free-speaking. At playground students joining me do walk with music on cellphones as one student lists "She" as helpful in English words for song.

CHRISTMAS

First holiday in Tongcheng with son, Mark and wife, faculty help us celebrate. A nice tree is our past shared greatest joy and family event. We see decorated tree as we shop together in supermarket.

Second Christmas in Tongcheng canteen manager is putting up large picture of Santa Claus on display in canteen's front window, December 2017, third term to stay taped to front window until fourth term ends in June. First Christmas tree I see in canteen is second December 25, 2017, lit up with tree lights appearing in morning. All Christmas day students put messages on small white pieces of paper canteen manager places on table under artificial Christmas tree.

So, I look at some of these messages to mention to Maggie who said, "Students write them to each other with warm thoughts".

One day, student carries artificial tree as if taking tree to dormitory room.

Students bring gifts to me to class like stuffed Santa Claus from Stephanie, ten-month student assistant, and sits on small square table to enjoy while eating home-cooking or illustrate memories, write verses or visit on internet until June. In classes, students may choose to share happy wishes in English words, take cellphone photographs or offer small gifts not unlike letter written in English to me on student notepaper given in English as foreign language class to enjoy in December for second Christmas.

Dear Maureen

I haven't writing letter to anyone for a long time. And it's really uneasy for me to express my feeling to you! Though there would exist some mistake in my letter, I still want to send my wishes to you and sincerely thank you for company. (If I can, I would hug you right now if you don't mind.)

Sorry for my careless, I can't remember the accurate date of our fi_st meeting, it's really quite a long time. Sometimes we may be distracted during you class, sometimes we may be too noisy, and we may behave clumsy, but we always respect you and we'll try to speak less Chinese in your class.

You had provide tremendous opportunities for us to improve our oral English, but some of us may lose it and be attracted by something else. And I want you to know that you were always playing a significant role in our process of English earning. (We do spennd some good time together.)

It's 1oçlock, a cloudy day in December, I'm staying at my dormitory and writing this letter to you, and where are you at the same time? I don't know. But I hope that you could stay healthy and always has good things occur to you wherever you are.

It's no doubt that there must be some English language practice in my vacation. I hope that I could have a wonderful vocatioi and I wish you the same.

Ooh, it's time for us to take class. And I want to emphasis on one thing that no one "deserves a bigger thank you than you, one letter is hardly enough to show our gratitude. Thanks for being such as great teacher!

Yours,
Haley

EARTH DAY

April 22 is becoming topic to discuss in conversational English lessons in classrooms. After returning to Tongcheng, Stephanie, student assistant, is telling her class of English as foreign language students, and in walk accompanying me to evening classes, Stephanie organizes her friend and herself to go about collecting and disposing of garbage they see on campus she is offended with to celebrate this day. While at playground in our fourth term in Tongcheng, witness students in small group planting trees across avenue in view atop lagoon bank on this International day.

BANKS FOR FINANCES

After arriving in Tongcheng in August 2016, I try to use my Hangzhou bank card at local banks. In Hangzhou, Lynn takes our small group of new foreign teachers to Merchants Bank to set up new accounts and deposit funds brought with us. Along streets in banks in Tongcheng guards ask me to leave. Joanna, first sophomore student assistant, tells me English ATM portals are installed at most banks. In next days deciding to ask for help at Bank of China I see on my first tour of Tongcheng with Annie and Sherlock begins new banking, valuable relationship. Bank is recommended by other new foreign male teacher in Hangzhou when we walk with Lynn, our employer adviser, day after both of us arrive in China. Tongcheng Bank of China bank clerk tells me I must travel to Anqing, one hour away, to use Hangzhou Merchants Bank ATM bank card. Bank clerk looks up addresses of banks in Anqing for bank card. I went back to my apartment to text Maggie and email Lynn in Hangzhou. Lynn speaks with college administration and bank staff. Maggie agrees to come to Bank of China with documents disclosing I am employee. Lynn discovers I must take out new account at Tongcheng Bank of China branch, and many documents including my passport will be used to open account.

Bank of China bank branch issues me second bank card after Maggie completes employee reference from college for pages of paperwork only written in Chinese. I return to Tongcheng Bank of China with Joanna student assistant help to translate and complete application for bank account written in Chinese. Second bank card from Tongcheng Bank of

China issues is to make withdrawals. Now I am able to withdraw cash to pay canteen to add funds to meal card to pay for meals, for example. At Bank of China ATM I see balances from Hangzhou employer's bank deposits for my monthly employee pay cheque deposits into Hangzhou Merchant Bank but I have to keep two bank accounts. New Tongcheng Bank of China bank card will allow me to confirm my bank balance from system of cooperating banking companies. Before departing Tongcheng, I transfer all my income to new Tongcheng Bank of China bank account for transfer to foreign exchange to bank of choice in my country by Tongcheng bank clerks.

Thank goodness cash reserves are growing in new Tongcheng Bank of China account to pay dentist at private clinic to repair broken tooth. One Friday evening in canteen, quiet and alone, while eat squash congee and steamed buns, back molar tooth falls into my congee. After texting Maggie of health issue, Maggie arranges to visit hospital next day, attending doctor patches break and cautions Maggie as needing personal care from home country. Next week, Maggie finds private clinic, appointments are arranged and dental work begins. Police officer arrives for first appointment, looks at dentist's schedule and departs with dental costs much less than home country dentistry. Dental work is success, dentist speaks little conversational English and students and Maggie are always attending appointments we walk to from college in after class time hours.

FIRST AND SECOND APARTMENTS AND MISSING TONGCHENG

Bathrooms in both apartments are modern with flush toilets, sinks and large open shower areas. Toilets, sinks and automatic washing machines are in shower area in first apartment with tiles on bathroom floor and walls of open stall. Second apartment's bathroom is fixed-up with new white tiles and brand new modern flush toilet, window facing apartment courtyard and door. Similar automatic washing machine to first apartment sits outside next to counter and large laundry porcelain sink with running tap water. Sponge bathing is method of washing myself or underwear in blue basin in front of portable heating fans as apartments and showers are too cold in both unheated apartments either to dry clothes or personal hygiene during colder seasons.

Illustrating scenery in hours of relaxation on washed used coffee filter papers is new craft to begin in first apartment and to store used coffee filter papers with my suitcase and drying rack in Hangzhou earlier in June before departing and returning to China and Tongcheng. Same small square table from first apartment moved to second apartment is for times to sit to draw with crayon and visit in video chats with family members.

FIRST APARTMENT

After arriving in September 2016, I sit near open dining room window to view sunset and bright moon over shadow of darkened mountain and enchantment after arriving in remote, subtropical area of palm trees in Province of Anhui. More than once as I sit admiring deep blue of evening skies under rising moons, salamanders crawl through broken screen narrow frame at top of heavy bright blue door leading to porch startling me or crawling through one large hole in bottom of cupboard under stainless-steel sink in kitchen.

Beeping in first apartment kitchen continues from heating element above refrigerator. Maintenance man tries to adjust temperature on large rectangular shaped heating appliance many times after complaints for hot water for shower are made from myself to Maggie. On warm September evenings, one bird flies into open sliding cloudy glass kitchen windows. I find bird next morning when I open window but mistook bird chirping evening before for heating appliance beeping. Next week after Moon Festival celebration at Maggie's parents home, Maggie brings maintenance man to apartment to move refrigerator. Maintenance man asks Maggie for help to move refrigerator to dining area of apartment. I begin to enjoy hot water showers. Heating radiator on wall above refrigerator in corner of kitchen begins to function as hot water begins to flow for showers after moving refrigerator to dining room. Electric kettle is filled with water from sink of first apartment's traditional kitchen at stainless-steel sink in corner and heated in large dining-room where only plug-in is located. Water is boiled for making green tea, drinking water and to sterilize my toothbrush often.

Long black shiny kitchen counter, lively with bright royal blue cupboards and large stainless steel sink at corner wall with running tap water features view of college academic buildings, dotted palm trees growing and sunsets behind western side of mountain. David advises to shut all windows when leaving first apartment. In early spring blossoms on small tree nearby in front of kitchen windows are pretty pink mingling with palm trees waving.

Faculty invite me to meet Headmaster Wu at formal dinner in autumn. David comes to first apartment to walk with me to small blue car driven by College President Shen. Card games are held prior to meals at most of these faculty meals. At first official meal, Headmaster Wu sits to my right at round table and at all our later suppers or lunches together in coming months and following year. He tells me he lives in first apartment in earlier times and closes down building from experiences with mice keeping him awake all night. Headmaster gives me flowers and gift-wrapped framed print at faculty meal.

"Waterway is street," Headmaster Wu said as he points and guides me through print with Maggie's English translations, who sits to my left. "Community waterways similar to canals are methods to leave and return to local homes in boats shown in print," Headmaster Wu said. Outside restaurant, after supper as David and I stand waiting for driver of car, David looks to me and motions across street to buildings and says this area of Tongcheng is growing and we are standing near new building development.

David walks me to apartment and, as we open front door an odour is offensive said, "mouse".

In my search of apartment next day find dead mouse in sliding, tall, open window in dining area next to table, left and went downstairs to walk across parking lot to row of administrative offices and college teachers' offices to ask for help.

Male teacher comes to apartment to help is asking for paper tissue and takes dead mouse off window frame to dispose outside first apartment, and so I said, "get mouse inspected."

Later in February 2017, in early evening, sizzling sounds across wall and ceiling of bedroom scare me while resting in bed at eight pm and planning next day's and week's lessons. Noises up and down wall never stop. Door to bedroom I now close and stuff clothes underneath door. I text problem to employer adviser, Lynn, in Hanghzou, and she tells me to stay in bedroom where I begin to use small pail for toilet to empty in morning in bathroom toilet. Lynn complains to college administration of problem and decision will be made if I continue to live in apartment. Noises continue for days in March until Dean of Maintenance comes to inspect apartment and notices tall, open window next to small, square table in dining area. Dean closes window and said, "Keep window shut, no cooking." Maggie standing beside me said, "I am allowed to stay in apartment."

Maintenance man standing nearby said, "Rodents are squirrels from mountain."

Next week on Sunday as mopping floor and as odour of mouse continues move refrigerator to see dead mouse caught underneath between floor and refrigerator. Mouse is avoiding traps set by maintenance man bringing for to put around apartment. Traps are flat black sticky six by ten inch traps opening like large occasion cards. Student assistant, Joanna, said, "Traps work well with poison, and I went to hardware store to buy poison."

Joanna mentions mice are problems and scare students in her dormitory bothering students in their room. I text Joanna I find dead mouse and ask Joanna to help. Joanna comes in next hour in nice dress and coat, looks at dead mouse and asks me to get some paper or tissue. Joanna moves refrigerator to remove dead mouse and we walk together outside to garbage can and Joanna throws out dead mouse and said, "Joanna how grateful I am,"

Joanna said, "I am happy to help."

Sizzling sounds going up and down walls and across ceiling as laying in bed in early evening stop. I text Lynn in Hangzhou mouse is found, issue is resolved and she is relieved and says to use apartment's bathroom in evening.

Large, heavy, royal blue door to right after opening stainless steel apartment's front door to apartment porch, leads to large dining area with small square table and wooden chairs next to narrow, tall window facing mountain's west view. In autumn or spring, varieties of trees resemble pine branches growing to mountain's summit are mixing with leaves changing to autumn yellows and reds show new growth and spring blossoms. Dining room's heavy blue door with engraved hardware is opposite same tall blue door to bedroom and double bed with wooden headboard. Large shiny, dark-brown wooden desk, holding college's desktop computer allowing me to connect Macbook Laptop and Ipad with remote access inside first or second apartments, is moved to second apartment. Tall cupboard and wardrobe to hang clothes sits in corner. Cupboard with two glass doors on top and two cupboard doors on bottom to keep my clothes for three seasons sits beside wide curtained window. As paperwork to stay in Tongcheng takes a few weeks, I unpack in early October when Permanent Resident Permit is complete at Tongcheng Exits and Entrances Bureau. All personal items such as photographs are kept behind tall, narrow glassed windows of cupboard with clothes below or hanging in corner cupboard for weather changes and next seasons.

Undoubtedly, Dean of Maintenance sees me bring shopping bag to apartment later on in May as I walk uphill to apartment and he leaves his office short distance away in row of administrative offices across parking lot from first apartment. Dean of Maintenance, tall and stocky with black hair and serious, kind expressions, walks toward me to ask to look in my bag as I assure him of food and shake my head sideways to cooking food.

SECOND APARTMENT

On sunny day in June near completion of ten-month contract, David walking to his office in academic building and leaving apartment is stopping his walk as I am leaving building of apartment to walk to next class. David said, "At meeting with administration I spoke up to ask for apartment a tenant is vacating to reserve for foreign teacher."

I said, "I share belief I may return to Tongcheng and college. I am very grateful."

On another occasion shortly before departing Tongcheng in June after ten months living in first apartment, David and Headmaster Wu greet as leave apartment and they walk together. In conversation mention my travel to Beijing in July to study skills to teach English as foreign language.

Late in June 2017, at farewell faculty dinner last evening in Tongcheng before departing to Beijing and training, Dean of Physics said, "bring skills you learn in Beijing here," and points down with his index finger in front of him as he sits across our supper table.

In reply to email note sent to Lynn, Hangzhou employer adviser, Lynn, is surprised by news.

Next morning as I am departing Tongcheng with Maggie, Maggie arriving at apartment said, "Headmaster Wu advises her my return to college is done deal. I do not want to do this anymore."

I said, "My luggage is too full so few things are left in bedroom wardrobe closet." Maggie walks inside to bedroom to take look.

After returning to Tongcheng in October 2017, Maggie is showing through new second apartment and provides key. Repairs to apartment are necessary for toilet, bathroom tile and running water to apartment and apartment manager is checking automatic washing machine as we tour. I ask Maggie by text for her permission to return to first apartment to retrieve my few things left in first apartment's wardrobe closet. A key is provided to me from student assistant to return alone. I walk uphill past fifteen foot magnolia trees in autumn to first apartment, now boys dormitory, to fourth floor. First apartment is empty and shoes and few clothes are left in same wardrobe in corner of bedroom location I left them previous June to recover for return to Tongcheng. Apartment's large, buffet-style wardrobe closet and wall of pine finished built-in closet cupboards fill large second apartment bedroom with large window and views of college buildings and gardens.

Accordingly, after arriving in second apartment, David arriving is for welcome and said, "A new textbook is for English as foreign language classes and never to correct students. What of my family's approval to return to Tongcheng?"

"Family are very proud of returning to Tongcheng," I said.

Days pass of using pail for toilet and running to canteen before classes and breakfast to public toilets students and faculty use. I contact Eva, my new Hangzhou employer's foreign teacher adviser, to request help speaking to college administration for completion of repairs. On an afternoon soon in October, Stephanie, new sophomore student assistant is accompanying back to apartment where David is neighbour and is preparing to leave on his very large gold e-bike. I stop to speak with him on his e-bike to mention work and plumbing for toilet so I ask David for new toilet be installed.

David agreeing sending plumbers bringing new flush toilet to second apartment and installation is complete in next days.

On the contrary, second apartment is much larger than first apartment and is among other apartments in building with six-floors and two apartments on each floor. Apartment front balconies and back kitchen rear views of college buildings are amenity in spacious second apartment with living-room and dining-room floors in shiny granite tiles and separate small kitchen with microwave. Same sky blue electric kettle is filled in laundry area with running tap water from large porcelain sink in long tiled counter and similar automatic washing machine and heated for green tea before classes in small kitchen electric plug with window view. Separate shower room is fitted with new toilet and three bedrooms with shiny wood floors are for my uses. Second bedroom next to large master bedroom holds small desk I keep class notes on and my luggage sits in floor. Third bedroom is location of all cooking pans students move from first apartment for kitchen and second plug for rice-cooker. Balcony is new warm, sunny location to hang laundry on drying rack from gift in Mark's visit last Christmas.

Small square table, desk and college desktop computer, electric hot plate, woks, pans and electric rice cooker are moved before from first apartment to second apartment before arriving.

Small square table, desk and college desktop computer, electric hot plate, woks, pans and electric rice cooker are moved before from first apartment to second apartment before arriving. Steamed rice is cooked in this second apartment bedroom nearby kitchen while meals are cooked in wok on same hotplate in second kitchen. However, I eat meals sitting at same small square table now in very large living-room that sits next to wall of windows dividing balcony with door to living-room. Second apartment's refrigerator sits in entrance area of this roomy apartment.

Views from balcony of college's main twin academic buildings six-floors of classrooms and offices stand three hundred feet past groves of palm trees and large gold sculpture sitting in front. Full size magnolia trees line street in front of apartment. From balcony and while hanging laundry glances are of magnolia blossoms lining street leading to former first apartment. Subtropical climate with palm trees is joined by large magnolia trees with blossoms of hot pink and white the size of basketballs, and are across avenue or up street from my glassed covered balcony. Views of jasmine shrubs with aromas from white blossoms in spring are views and to walk nearby to admire in college garden pathways. First jasmine aromas is from corner near restored female dormitory and in walks from canteen to apartments. Balcony windows open in spring.

At opposite end of large apartment from kitchen window, where I cook meals and prepare green tea before classes, is different window view of residents walking through passing to other apartment buildings or students coming and going to tall and majestic looking music school next door or student dormitories. One of two buildings of music school is like large dome with surrounding second-storey front walking balcony sitting on corner opposite welcome rock with green Chinese letter engraving.

Weather is record cold twenty-five degrees Celsius below zero in my second December 2017. Maggie comes to second apartment bedroom to inspect preparations I complete with quilts on my bed. One particular evening for instance, I attend college supper in heated restaurant at end of third term in December. David, Dean of English and now my neighbour on building's sixth-floor, brings maintenance man back from supper to second apartment to repair heating system. Rectangular upper wall heating and cooling machine about six feet by one foot is mounted on upper wall in bedroom in frosty cold apartment. David instructing said, "Stay in bed between two, three-inch cotton quilts on top and one, three-inch cotton quilt on top of mattress as second apartment is brutal with cold."

Maintenance man tries to program heating and air-conditioner system.

David said, "Will you trade your heating fan for new one he will bring to apartment?"

"Yes," I said.

Mark and Jin buy fan sitting nearby in Christmas vacation December 2016, and now is broken. Maintenance man takes old fan and returns with smaller pink heating fan.

December third term completion lunch with Maggie and faculty and administration on second floor in restaurant up street from college, Headmaster Wu is advising against any walking in snow. Huge snow ploughs sit at front gate and piles of snow line Long Mian Road during first snow fall in twenty-five years in Tongcheng.

Affording to pay for super great canteen meals, cooking for myself, work in profession teaching English as foreign language and living in first and second apartments without cost in Tongcheng are singular and joyous experiences. College network internet services are included without cost in both ten-month contracts in Tongcheng. After arriving in Tongcheng, Maggie helps connecting college desk top computer in first apartment to internet and brings college technician to set up college desktop computer to allow me access codes to college's internet network service. In few days after moving into second apartment, new student assistant, Crystal, brings her male classmate, who works at college, to connect second apartment's internet connection to college's internet network service.

Indeed in first tour of campus in September 2016, with Annie and Sherlock, we wander into college library's lower floor where sculptures sit at waste height and adorn front interior wall. I start to stroll past and Sherlock said, "Horse sculpture is for freedom."

Green jade sculptures in large animal figures sit on display to line front wall we view together. One Saturday I go to library to sit at long table on fourth floor with students familiar to me after returning to Tongcheng in October. I use library internet when apartments' internet waits for technician to connect. In return to Tongcheng, free wifi on cellphones with students ID at library is suggestion from freshman students, as apartment internet is waiting to be connected, but student ID is necessary. Supervised English sports magazine and book section on fourth floor I visit and view collection year before and return to library's fourth floor to sit at table in resource room with library staff friendly and helpful to access internet waiting to connect first or second apartments internet services.

Second of three free verse journals, *Free Verse China Journal September 07, 2016*, beginning after arriving in Tongcheng in early September 2016, write into original coil notebook bringing in my packing and useful for tutoring before arriving in Tongcheng. Writing verses to relax between daily class schedules is past common activity to me. After returning to Tongcheng in October 2017, third daily journal *Journal From Tongcheng* write into online application, and in notebook in my rest in evening. Internet Notepad Ipad application for writing is recommendation from son, Justin, shortly before departure as visit and while he insists wait in their home to complete authentications of documents and make visits to nearby People's Republic of China Visa Centre and Consulate close to large city.

PART FOUR

MONTH IN BEIJING

View of Beijing international airport runway is from airplane's window seat with low rise buildings bordering perimeter July 1, 2017. Passengers depart flight on outdoor staircase and enter building from Air China North's flight from Hong Kong. Flying to Beijing, for lust in heart above Great Wall looking like long chain winding through green mountains, is north from Hong Kong to Beijing, capital city of China and is located in the northern region near Province of Hebei.

Though arriving Saturday in Beijing is promise of one day touring Sunday before training for additional skills Monday in teaching English as Foreign Language. Oldest son, foreign teacher for last decade and half, recommends training several years ago to assist pursuing career as foreign teacher in 2013. Qualifying to attend with Language Link, and notorious difficult grammar tests online in spring 2016, evolve after accepting contract for English as Foreign Language work in China. Phone call from Language Link male staff from Beijing in August grants approval after grammar quiz in phone call. Two thousand CAD dollars wire to Language Link Bank of Hong Kong account in Hong Kong August 2016, for training is before departure to China.

GETTING TO BEIJING

Passengers walk through doorways of simpler warehouse-style building looking very grey in colours where one large desk sits ahead on left with sign for foreigners to depart China. Months earlier in August at sunny outdoor promenade of unique STAR downtown mall Lynn, foreign adviser and overseas Echo Education recruitment team member, walks together through tiles printed with names of famous celebrities in stars Lynn points out as we get-to-know each other after arriving in Hangzhou. In warmth of sunshine together sit on barrier while organizing time waiting with foreign teachers to apply for cellphone SIM cards at China Mobile store in Star Mall. Quiet moments are first chance to begin to discuss ambition to travel to Beijing next July eleven months later. Lynn said, "If you sign offer for second year contract to return to China company helps with visa."

Yet months later of early spring 2017, while teaching English as Foreign Language at TongCheng College Eva, new foreign teacher adviser replacing Lynn texts on Skype said, "Z Visa application requires returning to permanent home, and depart China before July 3 to return to work in China August 2017."

Replying in text on Skype said, "I must go to Beijing in July."

Eva texting advice said, "Easiest is travel to Hong Kong or return to home country to apply for visa to travel to Beijing."

Visa application requirements are stunning leading to days of research in hours at night after teaching classes with texts to Language Link in Beijing and emails to Chinese Consulate for information.

Meanwhile 26th June 2017, in evening, Tongcheng College's female foreign teacher adviser Maggie, and student assistant, Joanna, sit on each side at farewell dinner in nearby and familiar restaurant where meals are celebrated with faculty throughout terms and with family for Christmas celebration in months previous. Sitting across from Maggie and Joanna, Tongcheng College Dean of Physics offers gift box of locally grown green tea at dinner and said, "You bring skills you learn here," and points index finger down in front of his chest with pleasant enthusiasm. In reply to text to Lynn of details from dinner, Lynn describes surprise at news of contract to return to Tongcheng after returning to China for second ten-month contract.

In spite of departure planning for travel reservations on Air China airlines from Shanghai to Hong Kong and Hong Kong to Beijing, free hotel transportation from Hong Kong airport is attractive to register at Travel Lodge hotel in Hong Kong. Three hundred yuan each night of four nights is cost of Hong Kong Travel Lodge hotel. Invitation Letter is delivered in Tongcheng China Post from Language Link in Beijing to apply for new visa in Hong Kong along with helpful email planning lowest cost accommodations in Beijing. Both hostel and hotel are chosen in Tongcheng. List in email from training school is useful for booking reservation at:

> Beijing Lucky Family Hostel
> Dongsi Shier Tiao Xinsi Hutong 12 Hao
> Dongcheng Qu, Beijing, China
> luckyfamilyhostel@yahoo.com

Yet one sunny June afternoon after leaving classes and walking to canteen for lunch, Stone Sun, manager of hostel phones and texts cellphone in Tongcheng to confirm "boy or girl" for stay. One hundred yuan daily hostel monthly rate is lowest cost. College arranges for car with Maggie accompanying one hour car trip to Hefei for fast train to Shanghai. Maggie assists in speaking to clerks in Hefei to purchase fast train ticket in Hefei to Shanghai and walk together to security. At long staircase, Maggie calls out after clearing security for photo departing Hefei.

What is more Bank of China staff members in Tongcheng are helpful to exchange Chinese renminbi for Hong Kong dollars a week before departing for Hong Kong. Female bank clerk is familiar with foreign teacher working in Tongcheng. At podium desk arranging for teller to change RMB for Hong Kong dollars from personal bank account said, "I wish to visit Hong Kong sometime in future too and admire plan to see more." Soon teller behind glass changes RMB for Hong Kong dollars for spending money while applying for second visa.

On the contrary read in traveller's blog Sunday at Tongcheng College in spring 2017, of overnights and sleeps on benches at Shanghai airport to wait for early morning flights. Shanghai is worst in travel experience descriptions in internet blogs by travellers passing through Shanghai international airport and missing flights. After arriving on fast train in Shanghai 27 June 2017, from Hefei, signs direct departing passengers from fast trains. Attractively stacked luggage carts in row sit below airport signs and helps to walk through wall of glass doors with luggage and to departure lounge. In anticipation of long wait find small rest area of benches written of in travel blogs for overnight in airport with bathroom amenities nearby benches, more passengers waiting and hours later eat breakfast snacks.

More specifically deciding to check in with Air China airlines early next morning June 28, female travel agent looking at flight ticket details said, "You are at wrong airport. This is Hongqiao."

"I am departing at Pudong," I said.

Agent is pointing to go across Hongqiao international airport departure floor to speak to different Air China travel agent so run to service desk across airport's floor to explain flight to Hong Kong with Air China employees. Staff glance at details and motion to depart and point to street exit to take taxi to Pudong international airport. Running in direction travel agents point exit Hongqiao international airport through double doors to catch taxi sitting outside doorways in loading area. Three hundred yuan fare taxi driver offers to explanation of flight details. Assurances are to drive quickly one hour along freeway to Pudong international airport to be on time for Air China flight to Hong Kong. After arriving at Pudong International Airport, taxi driver stops in front and points at signs to entrances for flights departing Pudong International Airport to Macau or Hong Kong both domestic flights. Other passengers assist after entering airport offer front of line going through security and reach check in at Air China in time for departure.

Neither freshman student adviser's, Joanna's, description at Tongcheng College of fast train trip from Hangzhou, home city, to Hefei with stopover in Shanghai while visiting family or son, Mark's, description is with mention of two airports. Fast train station at Shanghai airport and travel between Hangzhou and Hefei is one brief conversation on teacher's arrival and first trip to Tongcheng 08 September 2016.

Oldest son, Mark, said, "While arriving in Hefei on fast train from flight to Shanghai from Seoul, South Korea and pre-booking reservation for fast train weeks earlier in December 2016, he and Jin must run to catch fast train to Hefei after arrival at airport in Shanghai."

STAYING IN HONG KONG

On the contrary numb with travel after arriving at Hong Kong airport delightfully find complimentary hotel shuttle. After passing through Immigration for Foreigner to visit Hong Kong and strolling to check-in at hotels' shuttle rides central desk, clerk in arrivals is providing round green sticker for identification asking passengers to rest in seats nearby waiting for shuttles. Excitement developing in shuttle ride with driver enjoying tour of vast city to Travel Lodge hotel travelling through Hong Kong to area of Kowloon like restful vacation. While checking into Travel Lodge, male hotel manager greets guests and offers meals at reduced prices in large modern restaurant at hotel with reductions' fee to pay in advance. In welcome female hotel clerk offers directions to nearby metro station and suggests name of private visa travel office said, "Chinese Consulate visa approval will take more than four days, and reservation at Travel Lodge."

What is more early first morning for breakfast in restaurant hotel staff give directions to spacious windowed dining-room door with hostess accessible from lobby to enjoy Western-style breakfasts or suppers. More directions from younger female hotel clerk guides walk to subway for metro train and walk to private visa travel office. While buying subway ticket security guard walks up to metro ticket machine said, "four yuan." After buying ticket descend stairs to take busy Hong Kong metro train. First-ever one subway trip is previous August with Lynn, standing nearby on crowded train advising new foreign teachers in Hangzhou subway travel helps manage time. Lynn points to details in map above automatic doorways with small green lights appearing in route lines arriving. Few blocks later, after departing subway stop, walk into Hong Kong travel agency.

Though soon in waiting area where many Chinese people wait, female travel agent calls waiting number, offers chair across from seat at desk and looks at Invitation Letter from Language Link for travel and education in Beijing. Agent refusing to complete application for any visa to travel to Beijing for training, decide to apply at Chinese consulate as agent nods possibility of approval. Outside travel agency urgency forces decision to take taxi to Chinese Consulate with costly fare. In English, taxi driver explains limits to travel within boundaries of Kowloon and drives to transfer location for second taxi. Second taxi driver stops in lane for arriving and departing cars at large building in downtown Hong Kong pointing to large white building declaring Chinese consulate.

Though walking into spacious lower level with wall to wall windows and two escalators to second floor, sign directions on second floor describe elevators to correct floors in multi-storeys and to Chinese consulate. At entry hallway is rope, curtain area with sign for consulate doorway to large open room. In small group of people waiting, female consular staff member advises in English and Chinese to everyone waiting to purchase passport photographs in photo booth on opposite wall in room before meeting with consular clerks. Across room photo booth sits. Our group of visitors wait for turns and consular guide's help with each photograph in photo booth pushing hair behind ears for photographs. Photographs taken, return to lineup and wait to walk into much larger room.

Yet male consular staff member is directing crowd of people in snake-like winding lineup distributing numbers to rows of plastic chairs. In large floor area numbers in lights are above desks for Consular visa clerks sitting behind clear plexiglass barriers. Waiting area is large to easily find seat near number-range to wait for permission to speak to consular clerk. Number is called to discuss visa with clerk within hour and walk to long counter with plexiglass dividers underneath flashing lights displaying ticket numbers. Pushing documents through barrier to Consular visa clerk sitting behind plexiglass, speak through screen in window reviewing application and Invitation Letter from Language Link said, "What is purpose to visit Beijing?"

I said, "Plans are training from famous Cambridge, England school in Beijing at Language Link."

Consular clerk said, "Deny visa application." Clerk returns Invitation Letter through plexiglass barrier and sets Consular documents aside to her right repeats, "No. I am denying your application."

Rising begin walk to exit. On left at front of large room of entry to application room is same attractive, five foot-six male Consular guide at snake-like line-up and walk towards group. With hand motions to guide in direction of Consular visa clerk explain application for visa to travel to Beijing. Consular guide nods agreeing and asks for pen and paper to write in Chinese and with translation in English on small one piece of paper from purse, and carrying from Travel Lodge Hotel with Room Number 701. Guide points next door, and said, "Chinese writing will help if need help for more directions:"

> "Chinese Writing' China Travel Service (HK) Limited
> Address: 2/F Tak Bobuilding
> No. 62 – 72 Cli Yee Street Mong kok
> 'Chinese Writing' 62 – 72 Çhinese Writing' 2/F"

In entry coupon arriving in Hong Kong travel document number stapled into passport states:

> "Visitor-Permitted to remain until 26 Sep 2017 Arrival Date(dd-mm-yyyy)28-06-2017."

Above inside red ink square China entry-stamp on passport page at Hong Kong airport is: "2017-06-28."

Though arriving at China Travel Centre (HK) next door after leaving Chinese Consulate, wait in hallway to meet with travel agents as office is closed for lunch sign shows. In office's small reception area with couple chairs and sofa, male travel agent listens to explanation of meeting at Chinese Consulate. He reaches for office phone sitting across and under counter with instructions to call Language Link in Beijing to discuss refusal of Invitation Letter. Language Link staff member in Beijing is upset said, "Sell place at training. Company has business licence. Most students apply for L Visa to attend training."

Following phone call with Language Link staff wait entire afternoon at China Travel Centre (HK) for second turn to speak to travel agent. Helping another customer standing behind counter five feet to right agent said, "Twenty-three hundred Hong Kong dollars is high cost to apply to Hong Kong embassy for multi-entry is solution to travel to Beijing. Return tomorrow to apply."

More specifically on first walk to subway from China Travel Centre (HK) to return to Travel Lodge become lost from small openings to staircases to departure ramps to subways. Help from older Chinese man speaking English and seeing home country flag pin on hat said, "I am familiar with famous politician, Trudeau. Left Toronto in mid 1980's to return to Hong Kong before Reunification."

He is kind to ask female passerby for directions from Travel Lodge Hotel's map to find metro train station. Hotel staff give directions on correct subway trains to China Travel Centre (HK) from nearby subway stations and daily walk pass famous shopping district of colourful vendor booths in long rows extending vastly down nearby street on both sides endlessly.

Yet roadways next day in downtown Hong Kong are under guard by military and President Xi Jinping of China is rumoured in newspapers to be visiting for twenty-five year Reunification celebrations with protection travelling in army vehicles. Walking from subway station is through boarded off sidewalks and areas to buildings to meet travel agents next day. On early morning schedule nearby Consulate and China Travel Centre (HK) Limited fast food restaurant, MacDonald's is bright and clean, more spacious with sophistication than any other to sit at table in dining area with cup of coffee and breakfast potatoes from menu. Hong Kong police officers sit across room nearby. Restaurant table clearing staff appear to be few mentally-challenged workers clearing tables alongside other workers. After enjoying small meal, tour around area with travel agent directions to International Money Exchange for Hong Kong dollars from Renminbi brought to pay hostel and for spending money in Beijing. Nearby are small convenience store and handy food market. Next door to Money Exchange waiting outside small business to open, closed restaurant is in darkness in window view of big screens with signs for golf games and screens for sports games visible to stand glancing through windows. Hong Kong dollars are simple exchange from filling in small form for clerk. Outside with Hong Kong dollars in purse take moments to look across street to park-aide and quiet streets as imprint of business details before strolling back to Travel Visa Service (HK) Limited in early morning.

Nevertheless, after arriving at China Travel Service (HK) Limited male visa agent accepts payment in Hong Kong dollars, rips up Language Link Invitation Letter and hands over counter application form and pen to complete application. While agent helps in completing application said, "What are chances of success of visa?"

Agent said, "Some risk for success of application."

Meanwhile later in break walk across pedestrian bridge adjoining buildings finding rooftop garden and rest area with few smaller outdoor patio restaurants with signs selling coffee and Cantonese food. At street level down nearby street, private school gate is open with students getting into black limousines parking with drivers in black suits standing beside vehicles on street. Students in burgundy colour uniforms resemble photographs from *NewYorker* magazine issue of private school in downtown Hong Kong where wealthiest families send children. Students stand together in groups smiling and speaking to each other on street outside large school's front tile courtyard behind wide, open gate entrance.

Moreover during walk back to Chinese Travel Service (HK) Limited in nearby strip mall, name Bank of China is familiar from Tongcheng. At front door bank guard standing said, "Sit in chair inside bank to wait for bank clerk."

"No. Bank of China bank card from mainland cannot be used in Hong Kong at Bank of China. Thank you for coming to Bank of China," said clerk staring and standing back from teller's desk.

Though back at Travel Visa Service (HK) Limited agent instructs return next day in final morning schedule in Hong Kong. After breakfast at hotel, subway to downtown and returning to visa service, male agent insists return at three pm. Twenty-five year reunification of Hong Kong to China celebrations are held outside on lawns in front of Chinese consulate building so find place to sit in shade on grass to wait and watch entertainment. Friendly man speaks in English to invite to sit and share shadier space with group sitting together. While sitting with group young white woman and nationals walks past on nearby sidewalk and street barricades. Across street is multi-storey park-aide and quiet time to watch entertainment with speeches and songs and to pull out small empty sugar packet and pencil from bag to sketch event as familiar moment in visit to Hong Kong.

Since returning to Travel Visa Centre(HK) at three pm waiting on lumpy sofa, mother and son nationals are taking passport photos, some apply for visas, and white business person is speaking to agent at counter across room. Customer turns to speak across room to ask plans for being in Hong Kong. Confident-looking wearing business-like clothes with gesture offers business card. Rising from lumpy sofa, walk towards man and receive card with man's name as member of Hong Kong Rotary. In chair nearby young white woman sits and stands to argue with travel agent friend is to help. We visit awhile in seating area and tells in English lives on mainland near Hong Kong city working in restaurant for friend as Hong Kong is too expensive. Young white businessman arrives near five pm and stands at counter for visa information said in English, "I am from Italy and start export and import business in Shanghai but visa issues to continue to work are more difficult.

I said, "My plan is to travel to Beijing for training in skills teaching English."

In truth near six pm travel agency's phone rings, male agent answers, listens and said, "Hong Kong Embassy calls. Visa application is successful." Agent walks around from behind office counter to walk across floor in front of seating area leaving visa travel office to retrieve passport from Hong Kong Embassy, returns within fifteen minutes with passport stamp into new passport page:

> "CHINESE VISA CATEGORY L ENTRIES M ENTER BEFORE 30JUN2025 ISSUE DATE 30JUN2017."

More specifically after taking subway from downtown Hong Kong in final warm evening June 30th, walk through picturesque shopping area returning to Travel Lodge hotel and pack for departure on Air China flight in morning to Beijing. In hotel's lobby next morning waiting for airport shuttle, younger woman arrives in lobby from hotel elevator accompanying child staying in hotel and is meeting young man. Shuttle ride to airport on coastline along harbour in ring of palm trees is across blue calm sea from skyline of Hong Kong. Pre-checking baggage at Air China desk with English signs proceeds quickly to walk into preboarding long security lines in huge stuffed room with people boarding for barely room to line-up at end of line of foreign and national travellers. Lines steadily progress to border agents desks. Next in line to speak to boarder agent with passport before crossing into departure waiting area, younger white male foreigner in front gets out of line drawing near border guard glancing at passenger passports and approves next passengers into boarding area to prepare for flight and wait. During walk to boarding through roped area with passengers, Hong

Kong money-exchange appears at last corner with younger man to quickly change remaining Hong Kong dollars to Chinese renminbi.

ARRIVING IN BEIJING

Beijing international airport opens into arrival area brightly lit to walk through roped-off path and younger male chauffeur stands at edge of rope with small white sign and rates written neatly on card, about ten by ten inches. Training staff email instructions to walk into arrival area of International Airport to find taxi stand for forty-five minute drive to hostel. Six hundred yuan is cost in sign for limousine service and more comparing to advice from Language Link staff. Limousine driver speaks and reads English and reads Lucky Family Hostel written on piece of paper agreeing to rate in card. Following driver to elevator to level below passing restaurant to underground park-aide, twenty feet in front walking to black sedan driver opens rear car door and sit on right of back seat. Chauffeur speaks Chinese on radio to company dispatcher evaluating rate complaining in English if charges enough because of afternoon heavier traffic and park-aide parking costs driver pays.

Nor driving down freeway, noticeably with older model dark green taxis, prevents asking and chauffeur agrees to stop at ATM machine. Off freeway as we approach city of Beijing, ATM is located in quiet location down lane. Chauffeur looks behind in back seat said, "We are at ATM machine and wait," as nods to ATM machine.

Sunny sky shines on Beijing in early July afternoon. Short walk is to exterior wall of building with ATM Bank of China bank card to withdraw cash from Tongcheng bank account to pay Beijing hostel half and return to car. "Thank you," I said.

Waiting driver said, "You are welcome," and starts up car to continue route to Lucky Family Hostel.

Close to hostel, we pass restaurant and grocery store and turn right where driver finds lane access off city street in early Saturday evening to drive down paved alley with narrow corners and tight turns.

Indeed in distant view after sharp right turn with homes and doorways on both sides of alley and cars parking beside their homes up against walls of homes is sign with Beijing Lucky Family Hostel. Colourful red lanterns with gold fringe braiding hang across front of hostel with couple of chairs sitting in front for friendly first impression. Lanterns are familiar in Tongcheng during Lunar New Years.

Driver stops in front, and receiving payment said, "Thank you," and retrieves black bag from trunk and departs.

Wearing back-pack and shoulder bag carry black bag to enter hostel where cold drink refrigerator stands on left of entrance to narrow room ahead. One thousand and five hundred yuan is in hand to pay manager.

"One hundred yuan daily month rate," manager said, and is standing behind lobby front desk, "is much lower than hostel charges for daily rate in peak season like July. Grateful too for cancelling the booking company online reservation from instruction in email and tonight checking-in to hostel adding costs to hostel."

More specifically registration forms and receipt for payment for half month desk clerk prints out 01 July 2017. Hostel manager leads to back of hostel on main floor to room with large double bed, separate kitchen area and bathroom with modern toilet and shower said, "only for first night in hostel."

After warm shower rest in double bed with white linen to study preparation training materials passing time in evening. Sunday morning hostel desk clerk meets in lobby early before breakfast to move black canvas bag to storage room near lobby until Sunday night. Ordering western-style breakfast is at lobby desk from menu with pictures and wait in small dining-room next door for waitress and meal. Out in lobby after breakfast manager stands beside wall for table display of local tours to Great Wall and describe plan to find location of training to attend first classes on Monday. Morning manager is same middle-aged man who explains in arrival night before reasons for changing rooms twice is due to registrations at hostel.

To help with directions manager offering city map and directions to nearest metro station he gestures away said, "walking distance and less than one hour to arrive. Location is familiar. Metro rates by month are less, for only staying in Beijing one month daily metro train ticket rates are fine. Four yuan," hostel manager said, "is cost to buy one-way tickets at ticket machines with correct change or with ticket machine making correct change for ticket purchases by passengers."

Smiling said, “thanks” and leave hostel wearing heavy backpack with laptop and Ipad.

TOURING BEIJING

Walking down same lane driven through evening before but now with hostel manager’s map, turn left leaving hostel, walk past at least ten homes when alley turns sharp left leading to T-shaped alley’s intersection with new main alley. Final right turn to short walk leads to busy city street for left turn on sidewalk. Across street two-story castle-like fortress stands with soldiers walking along second floor balcony. Korean restaurant and convenience store are open and sports clothing shop sell canvas shoes, colourful t-shirts, pants and shorts. Across second alley access to remaining one block and left turn pass very small grassy park with smaller park gazebo arriving at sign with name and number for Beijing metro underground station.

Moreover for next few days one soldier stands at top of long staircases leading down to metro’s ticket machines lining walls in underground stations. Ticket agent is selling tickets visible through glass ten by six foot office. Metro guards stand at top of arrival staircases. Metro station is very clean and with few passengers on Sunday morning walking down two staircases. Lighted boards above arriving and departing trains where doors quickly open or shut announce metro train arrivals and departures and stand nearby for doors opening to quickly enter. Metro train map of stops in green lights, similar to metro trains in Hangzhou, is above to exit through automatic metro train doors. After departing metro train Sunday morning, find escalator on ramp for arrivals with brief wrong turn in correct downtown station before choosing turn-style and deposit ticket to walk up long staircase to street level out of metro station in downtown Beijing.

Meanwhile hostel’s manager’s, Stone Sun’s, directions are turn left at top of long, wide staircase from metro train at street level to walk one block to another street with street light and pedestrian crosswalk with familiar walk light. On corner beautiful storefront with tall glass windows sits on street corner with hosts at doorway and small tables in large open room reminding one of social clubs. Well-dressed Chinese young men and women are arriving, meeting hosts at wide corner doorway and sitting at smaller tables in large floor area. After taking pedestrian crossing to street corner with shop selling designer clothes, hostel manager's map guides turning left on wide sidewalk to continue and pass MacDonald's restaurant. Breakfast and coffee for few times in month are weekdays or Saturday mornings. Once in month in morning break, Wan Wei, training manager walks along street together as young female training student, who decides to quit her regular job in hopes of better job, insists MacDonald's cappuccino bar is regular treat. Wei turns down invitation to join us as must leave for nearby apartment or middle school through wide gate where cars and students arrive and very close to training.

What is more twenty-five written in numbers is on brass wall plaque on right Sunday morning in privacy wall after walking one more long block passing restaurants and opening to supermarket.

In good humour in Tongcheng, Dean of English, David Wang, at faculty dinner mentions at table said, "The most famous middle school one is in TongCheng!"

Brass plaque is beside front wide iron gate on wall enclosing large structure behind closed gate of see through bars and expansive large front tile entrance where cars and students arrive during next weekdays. Dean David Wang said, "Number one middle school in Tongcheng is school famous Chinese politician is educated."

Dean of Physics sitting at faculty dinner table announces with amusement said, "Beijing middle school is number twenty-five. In China middle schools are given numbers for identification."

Undoubtedly building with gold-looking brass frames in front doors is as Lucky Family Hostel manager describes building with windows and gold-number address at end of block. Front glass doors are unlocked to walk into building where lone guard sits at desk in left corner of large lobby. Building guard notices foreign visitor glancing without comment for right-turn on main floor and sets of elevator doors to seventh floor. Offices of locked doors on seventh floor are down, wide and carpeted hallway to training offices gold-frame glass doors on both sides of hallway opposite each other. Bathrooms and closed office doorways are in either direction. Departing quickly from seventh floor down to main floor walk past guard.

On the contrary after leaving building walking tour around block after crossing quiet wide street from building begins with meeting younger man, who tries to walk alongside, tells art painting sculpture is at nearby gallery art show today. Shaking head sideways repeatedly speak little and decline. Soon artist turns around at end of block to walk away in different direction. Artist describes unique art sure to impress. In pleasant sunshine and warm air, two left turns lead past famous luxury hotels on both sides of street and past smaller fruit market with young couple buying fruit. Second fruit market appears and later in month buy large section of local exotic jackfruit as clerks speak only Mandarin. Few people wander around large block Sunday morning circling around. Down same long staircase to rows of ticket machines for first time, ticket agent in small office with windows sells return ticket with time of purchase to departure ramp down long staircase.

In spite of departing at wrong metro station past Lucky Family Hostel in area with small clothing and food stores like deep spaces and sizes of bedrooms in late Sunday afternoon, walk back to Lucky Family Hostel with map hostel manager provides and soon meet Chinese tourists. Friendly tourists to Beijing, noticing Western country's flag pin on hat, offer introductions in English and describe area north and inland away from Beijing and wait to depart to visit Western country's world famous event, Calgary Stampede. Visiting group begins to cross street in pedestrian crosswalk and walk with them. On right large castle fortress viewing earlier in walk from Lucky Family Hostel to metro train station seems familiar. In front of castle-like complex memorial plaque describes Chinese princess at seventeen marries, moves to Peking City now known as Beijing, and gives palace to people of China. On left wide front gate opens to very large looking buildings. Inside gate near front is office building. While passing open front gate, small car arrives with female passenger. Past front entrance is street light leading across street from Palace to familiar street from earlier departing hostel.

On the other hand high walls and sculpted tops and balcony, where often guards patrol and enclose interior of official palace passing every morning to take metro train to downtown Beijing, is short time to enjoy being near history of Chinese princess. At intersection near Lucky Family Hostel, father and daughter are biking and he looks sideways to young girl to guide her through lighted intersection. Traffic lights are identical to Western-style traffic lights with green, amber and red lights and walk lights for pedestrians. After crossing intersection, and walking on familiar street in late afternoon, to right Korean restaurant is busy with young customers and brand clothing store sells variety of sporting clothes to customers. At entrance to alley row of public toilets on left with doors to either elevated or squat toilets line alley's wall for handy landmark to turn right down alley to hostel.

LIVING-A-MONTH IN LUCKY FAMILY HOSTEL

Fifteen to twenty-five yuan buys breakfasts and suppers of western style food orders at hostel's main front desk where each order is made with desk clerks and paid for from menus with feature photographs and descriptions each morning and evening before leaving for and returning from training. Both small thick wood polished tables with stools for two line wall right of doorway and larger rectangular tables with four to six stools line wall left of doorway in comfy restaurant. One large window looks into street alley in narrow room of hostel restaurant. Television sitting on upper ledge is to left of entrance doorway often showing Beijing news and available to guests by remote control sitting on nearest table.

Though unless front desk orders, "Four pm is early," lobby clerk said, "but check. Cook lives and cooks for many nearby," and clerk points to back of hostel.

Clerk walks out rear doorway to adjoining building to arrange meal order with cook returns said, "Fine cook makes your meal."

After meal clerk helps collect smaller black canvas bag with clothing and effects from storage room, selects room key and shows dormitory shared co-ed room with four bunk beds and individual lockers across hall on main floor from dining-room. Settling into first top bunk from doorway in four person co-ed dormitory room with Ipad in late afternoon rest and prepare to sleep on top bunk bed at five o'clock for early start to Monday. Waking early before six-thirty next morning is time to pack-up and empty dormitory room's locker on wall opposite double bunk beds where three other guests sleep. Pairs of canvas shoes are lying in front of lockers and quietly clear locker of small canvas bag. Carrying bag wear backpack for laptop and Ipad and shoulder bag to front desk clerk to store canvas bag in locked room Monday morning and order breakfast.

Most important six to six-thirty in morning each week day is schedule to find shared bathroom empty on second floor. Down lengthy hallway in soft yellow paint, original oak-look railing follows stairs to main lobby. Hostel is mostly quiet in early morning with occasional backpackers as ordering breakfast at front desk and wait for meal service in dining-room next door. Many mornings dining-room is full with travellers. A lot of European families, known from languages spoken, are staying. Food is tasty and always hot for breakfast or supper choices with french toast, eggs, ham or bacon. Sunday training offices close and eat breakfast slightly later. Although during walks to metro trains pass few residents, and inside one home nearby to Lucky Family Hostel elderly woman sits quietly in near darkness close to open doorway with second woman in background. Across from elderly lady's place, residents arrive at large two-story traditional-style home with upturned eaves on roof and fancy doorway and looks similar to Lucky Family Hostel before becoming affordable to visitors. Mostly homes in alley are low rise with concrete exterior walls and cars stuck like velcro.

Meanwhile after returning to Lucky Family Hostel from training classes first day, Monday, front desk clerk hands over key to private room, retrieves canvas bag from store room and shows new permanent location for one month in upstairs private room after sleeping in two other rooms Saturday and Sunday. Private new room is comfortable with double bed and room to walk on one side with small bedside table and lamp. Portable television is sitting on waste high stand not in use with lower shelves to left entering doorway and two foot space in front between bed for black canvas bag to sit. Plugin for hair dryer is on wall near tall clothes pole on right entering room useful to hang larger towel to dry after daily showering at night. Before departing for China in 2016, youngest son provides airline issue plug-converter which works in both Tongcheng and Beijing to plug in hair dryer oldest son brings for Christmas in Tongcheng in 2016 when he said, "is there any desirable gift?"

Shelves are useful to store training books, class notes and clothes. "Food is not allowed in private room," desk clerk said. "The room is cleaned and bed linen changed weekly."

Towels are brought in luggage from Tongcheng. After returning Monday to hostel and settling into hostel's private room, after supper Maggie's email arrives. College Human Resources turns down Maggie's request for other training funding and joining together in Beijing.

Nevertheless, shared well-used bathroom on second floor with modern toilet and toilet paper, small sink and cubicle shower with glass doors is cleaned daily, and window is open for airing bathroom. View out bathroom window looks into small outdoor courtyard. Wide staircase with original wood railing leads upstairs from lobby to second-floor hallway. Second-floor rooms are on either side of lengthy hallway to one shared-bathroom at end of hallway in corner on right for second floor guests. Daily walk from lobby to private room is up wide but very old wooden staircase to end of hallway. Left at corner, from shared-bathroom down balcony-like short hallway, looks over railing to exterior door. Outside is alleyway in front of Lucky Family Hostel. Seldom waiting for shared-bathroom in early mornings, evenings are much busier with second-floor guests using shared bathroom to shower and prepare to rest for night.

Most important room key is left with clerk each morning to retrieve each evening after returning from training. Breakfast orders at front desk with early morning desk clerk at six-thirty each morning allow ten minutes to prepare most days to serve in small dining room next door and enjoy idle pleasure. After breakfast walking each morning down alley is tantalizing fifteen minute warm summer's walk to metro station. Twenty-five minutes is one-way metro train morning trip, walk few blocks and arrive at training offices nearing eight o'clock in downtown Beijing and leave training schedule at four to five in afternoon. Hostel is quiet in evening to study in room at night.

In truth in park area in front of metro station from Lucky Family Hostel, small gazebo sits for casual relaxation but man is sleeping on bench inside many different days of week. On benches and chairs nearby subway entrance, people visit together playing cards with similar card deck with fifty-two playing cards in deck of four suits laughing together on warm evenings but more so on any Saturday evening in July in calming fashion. Nearby is large concession-style bakery. One warm Saturday evening, returning from downtown Beijing to work on assignments at Language Link, buy best-tasting sweet bakery treat imaginable to carry and eat in fifteen minutes returning to Lucky Family Hostel down narrow lane-way alley.

Yet during breakfast one July morning sitting nearby at long larger table, male white traveller sits by himself near restaurant's window and facing all guests speaks to tell tries restaurant on street at entrance to alley to hostel but to turn right and few businesses away on street at entrance. Tourist is younger and speaking English said, "I use pictures behind counter in restaurant to order meals and food is alright."

Sitting at next large table said, "Thanks! I'll take a look."

Later nearer month's end during walk from metro train walk short distance to right out of alley, find restaurant open with menu pictures of local food and near bank with ATM but decide to return to hostel. Many travellers dining in hostel's restaurant include parents and grown children, and groups of travellers.

Since near end of month while at front desk to order meal Saturday morning, slightly later than usual before leaving for metro station to travel to training offices, tall male resident of Lucky Family Hostel speaks to me. He often eats in hostel's restaurant where sometimes looks after his violin with Stradivarius printed in gold lettering on violin case. Violinist is often with daily younger hostel female clerk walking in alley together after leaving hostel. Particularly musician notices small country's pin on camouflage hat and mentions is familiar with West and cousin living in country writes wild fires are very bad. He plays violin in Beijing symphony but turns down seat in Victoria, British Columbia symphony and visits city shrugging said, "Victoria Symphony holds less interest to playing in Beijing Symphony." Soon musician from Germany walks in late afternoon with younger female desk clerk smiling with greetings and meeting in alley returning from training.

Moreover on Sunday, July 23, sit at large empty high table with stool to watch morning local Beijing news in Lucky Family Hostel's restaurant enjoying breakfast meal. Hostel manager, Stone Sun, enters restaurant to watch news and chatters casually. Standing nearby in doorway too watching meeting on television at Tiananmen Square in Beijing with President Xi Jinping sitting alone on large floor meeting with military officials sitting at long desk along front of large room.

I said, "Were you ever in military?"

"No," and said, "I am never able to obtain respected work in military. How about training experience?"

"Training and schedule is very difficult and alright."

In mid July and returning to hostel near ten in evening, younger female desk clerk is behind front counter but manager appears said, "Hour is very late."

After picking up room key from clerk speak said to manager, "Training instructor keeps late schedule. I will return earlier."

Nor weekly Sunday morning walks with right turns outside hostel's front door down alley with filled water bottle weights feels like Sunday's foreign tourist and choosing to turn left or right at alley intersection. Few houses down alley in opposite direction from weekdays, Sunday walks pass homes with various ongoing renovations. Turning left at alley's intersection, vegetable stores with boxes of produce sitting in front and small restaurants with few customers are in lane to left. Walking to one tall apartment building with artificial coloured flowers in window boxes on every floor is landmark to return back, turn right at alley intersection and walk to Lucky Family Hostel on left in alley. Alleys are connected like tentacles of octopuses inside main busier streets for buses and traffic. Down alley to right after departing hostel and after two right turns is National Photographers Association with famous photographs posted in large poster-size display cases outside in alley. One guard sits in small enclosed guardhouse thirty feet in front to entrance to building for National Photographers Association with double-glass front doors and walls of glass windows exposing large wide staircase and sculptures on main floor. From hand motions asking permission to walk through to enter gate enclosure to building, guard shakes head declining. Turning around to return to hostel, walk back down alley with two left turns through Beijing alleys on warm, sunny July Sunday morning.

Neither view of first fresh mowed lawn surrounding small gazebo park in front of Beijing metro station later in month's morning walk from hostel to metro train to downtown Beijing is particularly notable and interesting. In months before student Tiffany, first year English Major leader in English Corners and class monitor, speaks of dreams of viewing large, green, mowed lawns of homes in Western countries, choosing English name from famous movie, visiting Paris and in love with English as Foreign language classes. Grasses grow to fall to one side like very good haircuts in front of college buildings growing in gardens of jasmine bushes and stone pathways maintenance staff pick-by-hand crouching low to ground at Tongcheng College.

More specifically buying tickets for travelling on metro trains is either by automatic machines dispensing tickets with correct change or creating correct change. Ticket clerks sit behind six by ten foot glass enclosed offices to sell metro train tickets. Metro trains are filled to capacity and seats are hard to obtain to return to hostel at five in evening. Lineups for tickets are long with automatic ticket machines out-of-service in downtown Beijing metro station. Arriving in downtown Beijing is busy on weekday mornings in thick lineups with steady flows of people departing trains to walk up one long wide staircase or riding escalator to turn-styles opening after ticket deposit and up another very long staircase to street level. After twenty-five minute metro train trips from downtown Beijing, metro arrival station near hostel is much quieter walking up long staircase, deposit metro ticket in turn-style and walk up long staircase for fifteen minute walk back to hostel. Lighted lanterns in darkening afternoon in front of hostel welcome visitors with staff nearby to hand out room keys.

TRAINING IN BEIJING

One morning while studying at cubicles in same office another male student begins describing living in China full time with Chinese national wife, university professor obtaining Ph.D in Western city, Detroit. Meeting while working on university campus in guidance and administration, "Wife," he said, "took Ph.D in English but makes a lot more money in China and so marry in China and with surprise Chinese government even took passport to obtain marriage licence. Forced air natural gas furnace installation business start-up company is doing alright in city near to Shanghai where we live."

Few foreigners are often seen in mornings departing Beijing metro station. In downtown metro station same male white student, who is medium height with thick muscular body, is walking smoothly and quickly short distance in front like how streams flow to walk with people departing their trains. With animated pleasant look, student follows crowd around exit corner through departure turnstiles with Chinese national passengers depositing metro tickets. Second separate afternoon again studying in two side-by-side cubicles and chatting share experiences of two Shanghai international airports. American offers advice for travelers confusing two very large international airports and said, "One hundred yuan is fare for airport bus between Pudong and Hongquoi, but be careful because bus ride between Hongqiao international airport and Pudong international airport is three to four hours to either miss boarding times at Pudong for direct flights to Western countries or tickets on fast trains at Hongquoi."

Returning to Tongcheng, Anhui, China in October, two months later, information is useful to take bus from Pudong international airport to Hongqiao international airport for fast train to Hefei and car travel to Tonghcheng after arriving in Shanghai.

What is more Chinese national students speak of admiration to teach English as Foreign Language in location like Tongcheng, Anhui, as beautiful and subtropical location of palm trees and huge magnolia blossoms imagining as paradise.

I said, "English as Foreign Language is taught at Tongcheng College simulating conversations in original teacher-written exercises."

Two thirds of thirty-two students are native Chinese with remaining one third mostly foreign teachers from United States, United Kingdom, Australia or Canada and living in China. Two training teachers, from USA and Australia, speak as curious of large class sizes in college I said, "large as over forty students." Australian seasoned teacher said, "I am not able."

To clarify in meeting with American also standing nearby said, "Studying English as Second or Foreign Language before arrival in China describes large class sizes in some locations are forty or one hundred and more students or blogs of foreign teachers describe teaching classes in excess of two hundred students."

In spite manager speaking in morning class said, "I refuse to work schedule ends at nine in evening and begins at eight in morning."

Training assists in learning best methods of organizing class time and limits foreign teacher speaking-time in class to encourage students with more class time to speak English.

Indeed in training schedule one mature male Chinese teacher insists to younger male Chinese student with Chinese accent in English-speaking skill, career is many years to speak English like native English speaker and is essential for job. Explaining later he said, "Improving masters application to attend university in England," as we walk together to nearby busy 7-11 convenience store and standing together in line-up for meals, "Order two entrees with lunch."

At 7-11 white foreign teacher with private school on fourth floor exiting elevator of same building as training offices on seventh floor, is often friendly allowing space to pay before as we stand in line paying for lunch at check-out. Observing one foreign white male student make coffee with simple single-use coffee packets, student said, "sold at nearby convenience 7-11."

One-use coffee sets are simple gifts to bring in luggage to share bit of Beijing's lifestyle with second oldest son and youngest son shopping in last days in Beijing. Similar in size to Western country convenience stores, Beijing 7-11 convenience store is short walk from Language Link at 33 Dengshikow Street, Dongdan with shelves full of food choices and extras, cold drinks in refrigerators and lunch counter serving Chinese hot meals.

Undoubtedly Saturday morning in mid July arriving early before nine am at training offices to work on assignments, same young Chinese man speaking English with heavy Chinese accent from classes earlier is waiting in hallway for training offices to open. As speaking together said, "Chances of failure are less than one per cent if all assignments are complete."

Later while studying in training offices same, curious Chinese student asks in computer area on different day said, "Do you know of this place called Richmond?"

I said, "I know Richmond where many Chinese people immigrate."

He said, "What about another location, Saskatchewan?"

Agreeing to share email information said, "I know of Saskatchewan and will send information to salesperson to request more information."

He said, "I'm able to sell."

Email arrives shortly from Saskatchewan and to young man next day said, "Salesperson writes many opportunities to immigrate in Saskatchewan."

Near end of July one mature female, who is paid by training management to be student for foreign teacher's teaching-practice-times, walks up to reception at front counter said, "Will you stay in Beijing?"

"I will return to Tongcheng, Anhui in China," I said.

Moreover in late afternoon's final departure from training, walk into ATM in downtown Beijing to withdraw renminbi with Bank of China bank card before departing China. Walking to and from training offices to metro station pass by opening to small bank ATM inset to street on wall. Withdrawing balance is with excitement see air flight compensation, bonus and pay cheque deposits from Hangzhou employer from teaching English as Foreign Language at Tongcheng College also in notifications sent by WeChat text.

Since manager of Lucky Family Hostel arranges for taxi to international airport on morning of flight departure 29 July 2017, young female staff desk clerk meeting on arrival to hostel, often working at front desk, friend to violinist, hugs as wait outside. Attachment to young friendly female clerk emotionally is gratification for comfortable experience and mutual in our expressions for departure in meeting and thanks for month staying at hostel. Two hundred and fifty yuan for taxi costs to international airport in sign on wall behind lobby's desk advertises affordable taxi rates.

Manager said, "Pay costs to taxi driver waiting and before leaving hostel. No tip as cost includes tip."

Outside front of hostel and across alley, taxi driver waits. Female clerk said, "Good-bye" as we walk to waiting taxi happy departing wearing new lime green cotton shirt brought in luggage and charcoal slacks with same white canvas sneakers worn daily to class in Tongcheng.

Undoubtedly forty-five minute taxi trip on freeway to Beijing international airport passes deep pink flowering shrubs in grassy ditches, fields of trees and parks hidden from view with trees and fences for sprawling lawns. At Beijing international airport, departure flights are posted in vast screens in immense airport departure area. Western air company's, "Flight is on-time," Chinese airline agent said checking-in, looks through backpack and shoulder bags and weighs canvas bag, "Go directly to departure boarding."

Wearing heavy backpack with laptop, smaller shoulder bag with purse and papers and passport always wearing close next to skin and waste-line in cloth band walk though security. Leaving China through Beijing customs moves quickly through lineup passing through China's security with passport and visa with category L Chinese Visa Entries M from Hong

Kong Embassy. Border guard briskly stamps cancel on visa printing in red ink. With time to stroll about, wait in second-storey boarding area. Sitting on second-floor viewing deck is roomy and comfortable on plastic chairs to people watch visitors buying duty-free gifts on first-floor in famous brand shops.

REFLECTIONS

Yet later next month in plans for departure to return to Tongcheng in late August 2017, apply for Z Visa with Invitation Letter from Hangzhou employer. Visa clerk pulls out of notary public authentications and paper pile Hangzhou Bureau Work Permit said, "You do not know what this document means." Visa clerk pointing to Chinese written copy of Work Permit with English copy on separate piece of paper said, "Deny Z Visa application."

Leaving Visa office to walk down busy street to parked car at meter, drive away out of city to stay nearby with youngest son, Justin, within one hour drive of Chinese Consulate and Visa Services offices. In sharing texts with Eva, foreign representative in Hangzhou, discuss solutions to language issues in Work Permit documents from Hangzhou Bureau. Youngest son supports solving difficulties searching online finding Open House at Travel Services in city nearby Saturday morning. Together we attend Open House whose travel agent asks questions of British Columbia Justice Department authentication and Criminal Record Check said, "I know man tells he is without Criminal Record Check because denies such speed."

"I apply in home community's police office agreeable to rushing through wait times," I said.

Three month delay is with huge amount of police paperwork for volunteers with wild fires requiring criminal record checks. So pressing further on said to travel agent, "Visa Centre deny Hangzhou Bureau Work Permit written with English translation on two separate pages in one Work Permit document to return to China."

Travel agent said, "I will speak Mandarin to visa agent to remedy Z Visa issues to return to China." Paying travel agent by credit card Rachel sits across office desk said, "Friend is in need of foreign teachers and will ask teaching qualifications."

"Plan is return to Tongcheng." I said as Justin sits on left. Following week in early October new category |Z is stamped in passport and sent by courier arriving to youngest son's home one hour away and depart next day on flight to Shanghai, China.

Though we wait together for car to take us one hour's drive to Hefei to board fast trains after returning to Tongcheng in October 2017, three months after departing Beijing, thirty day category Z visa entry-stamp for permanent resident is expiring day before. Mr. Ye said, "What about plans after arriving in Hangzhou?"

"I will take metro train to downtown Hangzhou Exits and Entrances Bureau to meet employer's Echo Education representative," I said.

We stand at college gate together, as Dean Wang offers ride in Maggie's phone call asking for help, in early six am morning sunshine to drive us to Hefei for our separate fast trains. Dean of English, David Wang and Mr. Ye both said, "Do not visit employer's offices in downtown Hangzhou." Mr. Ye curious about Hangzhou said, "What will you do in Hangzhou?"

"Of course," I said. "Plan is with Eva and taking subway after arriving on fast train from Hefei to downtown Hangzhou Bureau of Exits and Entrances to meet company clerk to register as foreigner."

Mr. Ye, Dean of English assistant said, "I cannot manage metro trains. We will hire taxis in Beijing."

I said, "Metro train experiences each day while staying one month in Beijing hostel are helpful experiences to manage Hangzhou subway advice from Eva."

Though black sedan and driver soon appear at college gate and quietly drive together arriving at expansive and very tall multi-storey Hefei fast train station one hour later. Security guards review passports, visas and identifications before purses, briefcases, luggage and backpacks are scanned and looks at expiry date on Z Visa in passport and reviews entry-stamp into China:

"ISSUE DATE 17OCT2017 CATEGORY Z REMARKS Required to apply for residence permit within 30 days from the date of entry."

Mr. Ye said to security guard, "Not a problem."

Security guard allows us through to buy fast train tickets. Mr. Ye assists in guidance with ticket clerk where passport is shown for ticket to Hangzhou and buys two tickets to Beijing for school business.

Mr. Ye said, “Keep receipt.”

Fast train attendants check tickets on fast trains with passengers after finding assigned seating. We soon sit at different fast train waiting areas for passenger lines to begin appearing with red lighted signs.

PART FIVE

WIFE OF HEADMASTER WU

Hong Wei Wu, wife of Headmaster Wu of Tongcheng College, begins our cellphone texts after meeting in January 2017, and sent two final cellphone texts departing Tongcheng and parting near end of both two winter-spring consecutive terms in Tongcheng in June. Cellphone texts between Hong Wei begin 12 March 2017, to our final text 30 June 2018. Our relationship begins months earlier at start of winter vacation in late December 2017. We share texting information after our first meeting driving together to Tongcheng returning from Anqing. Headmaster Wu keeps an apartment in Tongcheng near the college and Hong rides with us in car sent by college to return after our day together in Anqing and location of couple's home.

In car ride Hong sitting in front passenger seat said, "What is email and cellphone information?"

Maggie is help with sharing information with translation sitting in back seat together. Messages are sent and receive on cellphones in Tongcheng, Province of Anhui, China. Cellphone is old cellphone of Lynn's, foreign teacher adviser for employer, in Hangzhou. Cellphone gift-to-keep contains messages from colleague Maggie, Hong, and three student assistants, Crystal, Stephanie and Joanna, as well as messages from Lynn and Eva from offices in Hangzhou whose availability and contact is essential.

President of Tongcheng College attending most of our formal college meals, and first meet President Shen driving small car to meet Headmaster Wu at official dinner in November 2016. Often President Shen sits to

Headmaster Wu's immediate right at our official meals, or on one New Year's celebration in restaurant near college, next to David's left as sit on right nearby. Sometimes President Shen is very casual and is distinguished looking taller man, and balding. Even checking-up on if meals are adequate in canteen, President Shen offers greetings during canteen meals in college canteen on couple occasions during regular terms. Until Hong's final text, spelling name of familiar man and identification of official president of college is clear.

TEXT MESSAGES BETWEEN HONG WEI AND MARIA

Maria is easier to speak than proper name, Maureen, in English as Foreign Language and becomes name in use at Tongcheng College with David Wang, Dean of English or Hong.

A. Texts from Hong in first ten-month contract:

1. "March 12, 2017
Foreign Teacher Maria: I will leave July 01 to go to Beijing for 1 month training.

Ms. Wu: oh, yeah? Why? Dear Maria
Received 15:42 March 12

Ms. Wu: I am missing you "black heart emoji"
15:46

Ms. Wu: Do you still come back?
15:48

Ms. Wu: This is a book I write'peatry
16:40

series of photos : 1,book 2. empty bowl 3. book

Ms. Wu: It is also I write recently
16:43

photo: book
Ms. Wu: and this
16:44

Ms. Wu: I wish you a happy spring
16:46
photo: Mrs. Wu and myself in January 2017 at lunch in Anqing in mall
16:48

Maria: I will return from Canada for a new term in Aug.
Ms. Wu: Great
16:54

Ms. Wu: see I send pictures
16:55
Me: Yes. Yeh!

Ms. Wu: ok
16:57

Ms. Wu: I went to see you next week, right?
16:59
Maria: Me?

Ms, Wu: I went to see you next week
17:02

Ms. Wu
Maria: What day? After 4 pm is fine.
Ms. Wu : ok

2. May 15, 2017
Maria: Thank you for a great and thoughtful gift of cooked rice with bamboo route!

May 16, 2017
Ms. Wu : hello, maria. it's a pleasure. How's everything? I miss you. Hope to see you soon.

Wish happy! "black emoji heart"00:16

3. May 18, 2017
Maria: I am well and walking 5 kms. 5 days a week. My journal of poems is growing.

17:20
Ms. Wu: good
17:22

Ms. Wu: I will to see you at Saturday pm.
17:26

Ms. Wu: wait me
17:30
Maria: Where should meet? At what time?

Ms. Wu: TongChen
18:11

Ms. Wu: at Saturday pm
18:12
Ms. Wu: .....blank text

4. May 20, 2017
Maria: Thanks for a great 'tea time'.

18:08

May 21, 2017
Ms. Wu: It's happy. Good luck!
07:17

Series of texts is ending from first ten month contract 2017.

B. Texts from Hong in second ten-month contract:

1. April 07, 2018
Ms. Wu: Dear Maria, how are you recently? I will go to TongCheng afternoon, I will

see you!
hongwei

11:29
Maria: Okay.
11:30

2. Maria: When will you arrive?

14:26
Maria: I am well.

14:52
Ms. Wu: I have arrived.

15:32
Ms. Wu: I am visiting WenMiao

15:33.
Me: I am in my dormitory. Shall I meet you?

15:33
Ms. Wu: Ok

15:34
Me: Where?

15:35
Ms. Wu: I shall call you after visit.

15:36
Me: Okay

15:38
Me. What time do you expect to call?

15:38
Ms. Wu: 17:30

15:41
Maria: Okay

15:43

3. Maria: It is getting late. I have early classes.

17:32
Ms. Wu: can you go to school gate?

17:46
Maria: Are you waiting?

17:47
Ms. Wu: Yes

17:47
Me: Ok

17:48

In 07 April 2018, decide to go to canteen to eat before meeting, and later wait in apartment for text from Hong. Leaving apartment about quarter to six in afternoon dress in black pants and jacket on sunny but still cooler spring day, Hong is waiting with others and cars at college on street on college grounds near front gate.

4. June 29, 2018
Maria: I am departing for Canada tomorrow morning. Thanks for the visit. I have enjoyed your friendship. The Qingming gifts were a hit with my family and friends. Thank you. I took a photo.

17:59
Ms. Wu: Dear maria, how are you. I'm very glad to receive your message. You're leaving Tongcheng for home tomorrow, meet your children, It's pleasant. I hear you won't come to China again. I'll miss you very much. I hope the two years in Tongcheng will leave you a beautiful memory. 923857368@qq.com is my usual mailbox. Will you write to me when you return home? Please often take some photos and send them to me, and I will often take some photos and send them to you. Do you use WeChat. President Shen told me that you teach English through the internet, and I really hope to learn English from you. Wish you a safe journey. Say hello to your family and friends.

I love you.
Hong wei
June 30th 0122

PART SIX

DEPARTING TONGCHENG

Long Mian River near Tongcheng

New Tongcheng College campus 2021

Tongcheng Teachers College campus and Library, apartments on right, Green Mountain behind Library

Guniubei Reservoir view near Tongcheng city

English as foreign language teacher stays only few weeks previous year Joanna explains during our walk at playground after arriving in September 2016. Joanna's photograph with foreign teacher shows male teacher in hug with Joanna smiling shortly after arrival with teacher's grey hair neatly combed. Photographs few weeks later are from another student with same foreign teacher dressed up as Santa Claus before foreign teacher returns to Europe for health. Later in April 2017, learn at faculty dinner foreign teacher two years before arrival stays in Tongcheng three years. Foreign teacher marries wife from Tongcheng, and wife and child join foreign teacher in Europe. A picture is sent of child to Mr. Ye, who brings photograph to our supper and colleagues discuss. During this faculty dinner in April 2017, foreign teacher known privately to faculty working at middle school is also invited to dinner and apparently is acquainted with foreign language teachers. At dinner, Dean Wang shakes head towards table and to where sitting said, "College will refuse to sign second contract."

Employer in Hangzhou and foreign teacher adviser, Lynn, offering second contract asks to return to China in January few months earlier. The invited foreign guest-teacher to staff dinner discusses seven years working in China, and English as Foreign language education and employment after arriving and sits to right at supper, and Maggie on left. American shares he marries divorced local Tongcheng bakery clerk with one son and family desire to return to United States together. He himself is divorced and mentions losses of employment as engineer so decides on overseas career with frustrating early morning middle school classes employer schedules. Couple own apartment in Tongcheng and American describes process of ownership of completing improvements for walls and homes with affordable lifestyle wife desires to hold onto even after departing Tongcheng.

One year later 30 June 2018, Saturday morning day after final classes is busy morning with packing up final clothes, clearing out and cleaning apartment's refrigerator. Large suitcase is shipped ahead of departure with winter clothes and recent gift boxes of tea and pack clothes into same black canvas bag, newer backpack and small, shoulder bag holding purse and papers for international flight. Decision before coming to China is to bring clothes to throw out or leave behind. Pair of white canvas shoes left next to garbage cans for anyone to reuse soon are gone. Plastic bags for grocery shopping in small markets or supermarket sit on low bench next to wall in front of small black marble table. Clothes to donate are put into six shopping bags to leave outside apartment's main entrance under large, shady tree growing. Tree standing close to sixty feet tall, like poplar tree, is place neighbours visit and share smiles and hellos in either Mandarin or try to speak English to their neighbour, college's foreign English teacher. Often laughter evolves with grandma encouraging small child to speak English too.

Leaving apartment stop in at main floor apartment in same building where college administrator lives with wife, grandchildren, son and son's wife. Administrator's wife, and children are friendly and saying hello often in Mandarin. The administrator answers door to knocking and motion with bags of clothes but he shakes head and points to left to take bags outside to place underneath nearby tree. Few months after arriving in January 2017, term one completion celebration with Headmaster Wu, meet administrator sitting across large round table at upstairs dining room in popular restaurant nearby for college's official meals.

At dinner Headmaster Wu and college faculty offer to pay for car to ride with Maggie, college adviser, to Anqing for shopping at city's mall and Headmaster Wu said, "Together go to mall to enjoy ice cream."

The administrator living in main floor apartment speaks no English. Administrator is first to arrive at end of first term celebration with Headmaster Wu in late December 2016, and waits at smaller side table in upstairs private room of restaurant. Maggie directs us to small table, introducing attractive middle-age man said, "Administrator."

Maggie translates our brief conversation. One year later January 2018, administrator's warm, smiling, friendly wife meets in concrete stairwell, smiles, raises hand and nodding said, "Wait", as walking by to leave building. Wife reappears with couple homemade fried pancakes New Year's Day said, "Happy New Year!"

"Happy New Year! Thank-you," I said and return to apartment with gift for later before leaving building.

So took bags to large tree fifteen feet in front of apartment's main open doorway. Ten yuan bought only pair of royal blue plastic sandals with British flag design to wear in both first and second apartments from small, rectangular shop crowded with merchandise on Longmian West

Road where owner often sits near doorway at sewing machine. After returning back upstairs to apartment on second floor and past main floor college administrator's apartment, took last glance around every room in apartment with solemn farewells to enjoyable home. Gathering-up black canvas bag packing with last of clothes, backpack with laptop computer and Ipad, and one small shoulder bag holding navy leather purse to store underneath airplane's seat in front, leave apartment in building where college staff and families live. Descending two flights of concrete stairs knock on main floor apartment, administrator once again opens door, and offer stuffed panda. Student assistant, Crystal, leaves stuffed panda outside apartment's door day before with good-bye note, Friday, last day of college activities and classes. The administrator accepts soft stuffed panda. We say good-bye in Mandarin, and turning towards open doorway walk out of apartment building final time.

BEFORE FINAL GOOD-BYE

Black sedan car with female driver is waiting for travel to Hefei Fast Train station in capital city of Anhui province. Female driver drives to meet new foreign teacher's arrival in Tongcheng in 2016, and accepts lapel pin of country's flag, waits in similar car. Maggie, sitting in front passenger seat, gets out of car, meets in rainy weather outside apartment said, "Do you have key to apartment for me?"

"Yes. Key is handy in grasp to return," I said. Maggie forgot cellphone so must stop at her apartment first. The drive to Hefei is one hour on freeway busy with traffic Saturday morning.

An hour later in Hefei driver parks and waits in large outdoor fast train station parking lot, and Maggie stands in line to help buy ticket in very crowded entrance to extremely large lighted board, like a bill board, of arriving and departing fast trains.

"Eight stories high and bigger than anything in Seoul, Mom," son, Mark, said in phone call after arrival in Christmas visit to Tongcheng 24 December 2016, after flight from Seoul, South Korea.

One hundred and fifty seven point twenty yuan is amount of fast train ticket to Shanghai. Twenty yuan is small gold coloured coin in pocket change for exact payment to hand to Maggie. We stand together in lineup and Maggie said, "Maureen, you should buy yourself new suitcase."

Passengers in line in front of us all seem to have suitcases with wheels.

"Is two wheel or four wheel better?" I said.

Maggie said, "Four wheel suitcase as chance of wheels breaking is far less."

"Admire very huge ticket and departure and arrival lighted sign," and said and nod to billboard-size brightly lit with lists above our heads with hundreds of booked trains.

Showing passport to fast train ticket clerk when we get to front of line Maggie buys ticket with yuan, ticket agent issues ticket and reviews passport. We left this area to walk outside to another doorway leading inside to departure area where security guards screen luggage, check tickets and passports and citizen passenger identifications. Although through security scanning quickly there will be long wait.

BLITHESOME PARTICULARS

Prior October 2017, nine months earlier fast train ticket to Hefei from Shanghai is booked online sitting on sofa in son, Justin's home day of Z Visa and passport delivery from travel agent. Maggie video chats hours before departure suggesting new schedule and will meet Maggie in Hefei with driver to return to Tongcheng. Chinese Consulate's authentication process for Criminal Record check and University Degree are taking longer than expected to arrive in China in late August, so accept Justin's invitation in weeks before departure to China for second contract to return to Tongcheng. Mid October 2017, after arriving in Shanghai on flight, stand in Shanghai fast train station in line-up called, "Change Ticket."

"Twenty-five percent loss but adjust time in Shanghai after purchase," I said.

Catching-up visiting after arriving in Tongcheng Justin said, "I'm sorry for cost."

Returning and waiting one last day in China is pleasant with sold-out tickets to people-watch waiting to board for trip to Shanghai, and airplane to depart China next morning. During our times in Tongcheng, Maggie shares career past and is permanent tenure employee receiving funding to complete Masters degree with requirement to return to work at Tongcheng College as English language instructor. In mid May 2018, near end of second ten-month contract as English as Foreign Language teacher, we speak together after leaving lunch at college canteen while Maggie walks with pink e-bike said, "Weather is extremely hot this spring. What of plans for leaving Tongcheng? Are you going to return to activities before arriving in China?"

"I am returning to other plans," I said as Maggie is crying this sunny hot day.

Meeting for lunch once a month with Maggie in college's canteen is common and weeks earlier in March 2018, plans are new to us to discuss future Maggie, said "Do you hear from Eva?"

Nodding in response said, "I hear from Eva. Can you help to speak to college's human resources to renew Z Visa to return to Tongcheng?"

Maggie stood up to depart canteen and shakes her head said, "No."

Alone continue to finish lunch in canteen. After meeting Maggie returning to Tongcheng for second-contract in October 2017, Maggie suggests digital pictures are helpful in class. Maggie said, "I got a new cellphone."

Early days in first contract after arriving in Tongcheng, sit together at table in first apartment with Maggie and discussing Motorola cellphone bringing abroad but unable to buy SIM card due to 3G issues. Bringing out Motorola to discuss, Maggie sits watching pictures of farms appear and changing opening Motorola with large symbols, and hoping to help said, "This is better cellphone."

Physical aides like textbook, and conversational English lessons are taught in new classroom location down hallway from prior location without internet connection or chalk for chalkboard. In June 2018, near end of second contract Maggie said, "In classes results are obvious with two student assistants, Stephanie and Crystal, speaking exceptional English comparable to classmates after duties as student assistant helpers."

Soon in two weeks after arrival almost two years earlier in September 2016, Dean David Wang asks Maggie to invite foreign teacher to dinner to meet friend, owner of Bluniverse Training School, and two of their teachers. The dinner is in dining room of hotel restaurant short distance from college. David, his friend and two colleagues play cards. Maggie sits on left and we visit with two teachers sitting to right. At dinner Maggie shows pictures from cellphone of fancy, new white furniture for new apartment. Coco sits on right, asks for cellphone number at supper and is official Bluniverse Training School staff member to call or text cellphone Thursday or Friday evenings to request attendance at training school Saturday mornings for next eight weeks. School will pay in cash at training school for two hours in English as foreign language lessons to groups of elementary-age children or attend western holiday student events, like Christmas and Halloween. Lynn, from Echo Education in Hangzhou, says extra work is fine as long as classes and schedule is outside of regular week days' teaching schedule.

After Halloween evening training school party and Coco's invitation, travel together in taxi to go to Deli House restaurant on Sunday evening. At supper Coco said, "My boyfriend is in military."

"What do you do for your vacation time?"

Coco said, "Who has enough money to go away on vacation?"

Coco loves Yellow Mountain, one of three important national landmarks along with Great Wall and Yangtze River and nearby at Anqing said, "Suggest you visit and hike Yellow Mountain because located nearby in Anhui?"

Hong Wei also suggests this hike only much later.

Coco tells story at our restaurant meal said, "Foreigner hikes up Yellow Mountain unable to hike down due to broken leg from hiking up mountain. He may even have been medical student. Isn't this funny as he hikes up mountain and is carried down mountain."

"The story is amusing for surprise ending," I said.

Coco texts or calls Thursday or Friday night to be at college's front gate at eight o'clock Saturday mornings to drive to training school. On one occasion, driver suggesting walk to Bluniverse Training School but sitting in back seat said, "I will get lost."

In field trip lesson, Coco meets at nearby KFC within walking distance to college. Coco buys lunch after we conclude our English as Foreign language lesson with training school students and said, "Please have coffee? Coffee is so unusual."

Regular chicken sandwich Coco orders is similar to Western-style KFC, and known as Kentucky Fried Chicken. Our English as Foreign language lesson is English words for ordering lunch, making change of costs with customers and services. Lunch and cash are for tutoring from foreign teacher behind KFC counter at cash register with series of student as staff members selling to students as customers and with preparation earlier from week in Coco's lessons.

Our final texts in December are curious about joining Mark and Jin to visit local bar, and Coco texting back said, "Passports must be shown."

Mark said, "Forget going to bar."

First Christmas Eve in Tongcheng 24 December 2016, when receiving Maggie's text accept invitation to party with friends. We meet Maggie with female friend at college gate to drive to training school for movie and gifts to children. Large bag of traditional sunflower seeds and cash are for attending. At supper together in restaurant before we go to training school Mark texts announcing arrival from Seoul, South Korea to Hefei said, "We are very tired. We will check into our Tongcheng hotel and will meet Christmas morning and go to party."

The drive to Seoul, South Korea international airport is one hour from couple's home in Bundang and after flight to Shanghai Honquoi International Airport, is additional five hour fast train trip to Hefei. Mark said, "One thousand yuan is very high taxi cost but Jin succeeds in negotiating outside fast train station at reasonable cost."

For one hour car trip to Tongcheng hotel. "Four hundred and fifty yuan is amount female faculty member suggests at supper for taxi from Hefei," I said.

The couple later sharing details of fast train trip from Shanghai to Hefei said, "We tour fast train and plan okay restaurant meal in first class."

SAYING GOOD-BYE TO MAGGIE

Passing through security departing at fast train in Hefei station is fourth time, once one year ago and now three times in past few months. 04 September 2016, first meeting with Maggie at same fast train station is with colleague Dean of English, David, and wait at Information Desk with suitcase, backpack, and bag. They arrive a bit late and Maggie carries small paper sign with foreign teacher's name, "Maureen"

Printing with felt marker is on white paper. Both are smiling with big smiles walking towards Information Desk. During first contract year in Tongcheng, Maggie's invitations are to hike many Sundays and occasions to eat together in restaurants Maggie suggests after hiking. Departing China with Maggie 30 June 2018, is like still moment or interlude, and final embrace. Maggie walks to hug at foot of familiar security to depart almost two years later taking photos, sharing quiet goodbyes and few tears together. Maggie turns to walk back to security gate. Turning away walk up long, wide staircase fifteen feet away and with recent frequent trips helps to make decision to ship large, heavy suitcase to ease travel schedule. Maggie is waving and while turning to wave female security guard is smiling and lets Maggie through to run to help ascend up staircase with heavy bag and wearing backpack. At top of staircase, embrace for final good-bye, and walk on alone to boarding area of fast train station as Maggie returns to security gate where security guard stands nearby.

"Maureen," Maggie said from security gate, "You are welcome to return to China."

Turning around for final wave to Maggie, our security guard is watching and smiling. Phrase is officially spoken invitation and hear from male student first morning back in October 2017. At beginning of second ten-month contract months earlier in college canteen early one morning buying breakfast at congee counter hear,

"Welcome back to China," said tall male student, unknown from previous term speaking- up ordering congee too on left with canteen server gazing at us.

Turning with delight speaking English said, "Thank-you!"

We part to sit at separate tables to enjoy congee from vast choices of congee either with or without variety of red beans and simmering hot milk on large stove at right-end section of canteen food counter.

Waiting from seat in row of plastic seats to watch families and students going on vacations in early summer. Brightly lit high ceiling and very large waiting area is filled with travellers lining up to go through ticket checking. Numbers on fast train tickets are in lights above each departure gate. As departure time approaches passengers begin lining up, and stand in line for awhile joining them. We pass through security gate in front of glass doors and stairways with agents checking all passengers luggage and tickets and take escalator or stairs down to outdoors and huge platform where sleek and white fast trains run in two directions separated by wide concrete platform. On departure and arrival ramp, lineups continue in waiting numbers for stratospheric white trains arriving and departing quickly country-wide. While lifting backpack to open shelf above seats accept help from passengers and black canvas bag is also put on shelf above and hold onto smaller shoulder bag with purse and cash. Back in Tongcheng apartment, practice lifting backpacks and bags is past-time for travel preparations. The seats are three across with aisle between two rows, and with luck for window seat sit next to mother and believe her son in aisle seat. In six hour trip to Shanghai rest in comfortable window seat. Mother brings out cooked steamed corn and offers cob.

"*Shi shi,*" I said. We three sit happily chewing steamed sweet corn with pale yellow kernels enjoying passing scenery of fishing boats and fishing from ponds, bamboo groves and rural workers in rice fields.

18 September 2016, on break from teaching English as foreign language classes, during daily three to five kilometre walk at college playground loud air raid siren sounds. Nothing happens nearby student dormitories and keep walking. Joanna, new student assistant, explains later the siren is memorial to Japanese invasion of China. In English as Foreign Language class next day ask students if they notice loud siren. Students explain in small group classroom conversations siren is to remember Japanese invasion of China. Violence of invasion is example of opinions.

One male student said, "I'll never forgive them."

Other students said, "Wish and dream to visit Japan in adventures after College."

At spring staff lunch in 2018, one and half years later said, "Is anyone aware of evacuation siren day before hearing while walking at playground."

David laughing said, "The siren is for an evacuation of building in earthquake drill. Are there any activities for the drill?"

Enjoyable view at playground is of building like an Opera House with walls of glass and dome and rooms of pianos student assistant, Joanna, describes previous year.

"The large music school do drill practice, students vacate building onto front parking lot or playground track, and we all stand still in one place at playground track for earthquake drill routine." I said.

In second ten-month contract, David and family are neighbours on sixth floor in apartment building and David calls or texts, even in late evenings, for alerts for extreme weather such as heavy rain storms, power outages, and noisy winds making windows rattle.

Poetry From China

Being Authenticate

I find myself troubled

As I enjoy each day

When I lose my way

So I recover by trying

The results can be a surprise

I remember going every

Week so now I still pray.

Helpful times we had

And I make the effort so carefully. Maulo

December 18, 2017

Christmas Not Christmas Eve

Even though the Eve was planned

With music from Christmas in Ireland

The location did not permit it

And for hours I was tormented.

So I stood my place

Ignoring the troubled one

Until I could manage

A reasonable choice.

Christmas Eve is magical.

December 25, 2017 Maulo

Sunday hikes in first ten-month contract are frequent on Buddhist's Mountain near TongCheng and arrive by passenger on Maggie's pink e-bike. We often park even in others' driveways and walk up mountain past homes located near bottom of roadway to mountain. The zigzag mountain road with fast cars and hikers strolling-up is lengthy and pass white stucco homes near green fields and as we make our way up mountain enjoy sunshine near trees like pine or bamboo groves. In view is vast east or west landscape with Tongcheng skyline or green mountain valleys in distances Maggie photographs. Large gated residence appears on left for monks to Buddhist Temple and new building is in construction on right for much larger, impressive new temple in large lot set into trees and promising beauty with flower gardens and lookouts to visit. Always hiking to summit, we rest at local temple.

One occasion after several hikes in warm spring 2017, Maggie is inviting friend and daughter to join in on hike. Before departing Tongcheng in friend's car, friend is purchasing cold drinks from nearby convenience store. Maggie asks for help in tutoring young girl in early teens hiking together up mountain road said, "Child attends public school, an opportunity she competes for, pays fees to attend, and unlike western countries where students attend without cost."

We park and hike stopping before top of mountain at building site with large concrete balcony with flower gardens nearby to indoor displays and sit on low wall at lookout in front of new building and restorations. Young girl speaks English learning enough from public school classes to chat as walking together up mountain. Maggie and mother sit on short wall of concrete balcony to temple buildings. Mother sees backpack hanging down back over ledge so suggests dangerous and agreeing remove backpack to sit together aware of steep slope below. Young teenager accepts invitation to walk through nearby open museum-like small building and flower gardens and museum displays enjoying casual English conversations.

In past times local citizens bring food packages to lone monk in isolation on mountain without departing temple and monastery on mountain at temple in roadway. Tea fields are planted in higher tiers of mountain where mountain's mists can reach them. Dreams of viewing tea fields in mountain mist from years past are in photographs manager shares working in tea shop in 2009. Maggie suggests climbing together up to mountain's second tier where mists ripen tea for picking during November 2017. Maggie checks if staff are in shelters with open doorways similar to fruit stands and offices for tea pickers but are looking empty said, "No one is here."

Tea plants in large fields are only few feet away to stare for few moments in chance to be near fragile small tea plants in fields. In long rows flowing down mountainside, small little thin plants like bushes are growing in dry-looking grey soil down field in many rows with borders on edge dividing up acres.

In March 2017, female, freshman student asks to speak in class during opening self-introductions and stands-up to share phone photos, speaks of weekend tea-picking with parent and grandparent, and picking tea from bush of fresh tea-picking putting in basket with parent in same week. Maggie counsels with students to share tidbits like personal dreams of their foreign teacher. Dreams are like sharing good recipes for example, and Lynn, employer adviser, explains too after meeting in Hangzhou in days after arriving in China of travels to United States months before to enjoy dream of Christmas winter season with snow and cold.

Poetry From TongCheng

Beginning Term 2

I got my suitcase packed

Ready to be organized and shipped

There are supposed to be 16 weeks

I am not very popular with my colleague

Who has become distant and difficult

So I may have to leave earlier.

English is popular

But the foreigner seems an interest

Scandalously. Maulo

March 3, 2018

REGISTERING TWICE FOR PERMANENT RESIDENT PERMITS

In following days after arriving in Tongcheng during morning in September 2016, Maggie requests first ride as passenger on pink e-bike to first visit to Tongcheng Exits and Entrances Bureau, very large multi-storey building few blocks away from college. After discussions with police officer discover travel to Anqing, Anhui to begin application is first step to register within thirty days as foreigner in permanent residency in Anhui province after arriving in China to meet employer in Hangzhou, in Zheijiang province farther north in coastal region. Maggie is arranging to travel to Anqing with three male college staff members with business in Anqing. After arriving at government offices and meeting, we must wait for processing some details and enjoy lunch of fresh fish at nearby restaurant. During lunch Maggie explains to avoid picking bones out onto plate but spit bones after taking bites of fish. Anqing Bureau issues receipt for passport and holds passport for thirty days until October.

After second visit to Anqing Bureau within thirty days later, we will wait for document processing and to retrieve passport with Permanent Foreign Resident Permit from Anqing Bureau. Maggie suggests taking walk along concrete viewing deck across street from huge blue Buddhist temple together watching multi-layer boats like ferries sailing with passengers from community pathway on bank of Yangtze River, third longest river in world and longest in Asia, and longtime dream to see. We stand together with calmly moving Yangtze River with clear view of width across flowing waters to tree groves on opposite bank.

I said, “Who is taking the large white boats like ferry-ships up and down stream?”

“Large white boats with decks carry passengers up and down stopping at variety of ports passengers depart to tour,” Maggie said.

Later in class introductions, students are loving and amusing with enthusiasm, excitement, and respect of such vast Yangtze river in students’ classroom confessions of Maggie’s counsel explaining one of foreign teacher’s lifelong dreams to Maggie earlier.

We wait to meet Maggie's hometown acquaintance with new child joining up for lunch.

Maggie said "I see this friend seldom. We are from same hometown."

A taxi arrives with Maggie's friend and we depart together in taxi. Our lunch is in bright yellow and comfortable restaurant where orders are made inside main front door entrance from large pictures on wide wall before sitting at smaller table in spacious bright room on second floor. First corn milk shake is soothing rich flavor friend orders arriving in pitcher and ask to share corn shake drink order as Maggie's hometown friend sits across table.

Maggie translates conversations said, "My friend is middle school teacher with very easy job."

Shortly after arrival weeks earlier and first Sunday afternoon in Tongcheng at hotel before moving to apartment Maggie arrives beaming in afternoon said, "Working extra-hours teaching English as Foreign Language at training school of friend this afternoon to much younger elementary school students on Sunday and enjoy helping friend at new training school."

The restaurant is busy and full with customers on second floor. Gold colours decorate large dining room. Later friend departs early from our taxi ride. Maggie tries to give her friend an official Red Envelope gift Maggie's friend refusing throws envelope into street. Friends part with hair-pulling-hug as waiting sitting in backseat with taxi driver. Same taxi drives to Bureau for passport and payment Maggie making on behalf of college. Maggie asks taxi driver to wait to drive to Anqing bus station for return trip to Tongcheng. In morning trip from Tongcheng to Anqing, Maggie arranging co-op taxi, travel with more customers travelling to Anqing.

Later Dean of English, David, tells and Maggie said, "David's advice is taking chance to use bus to return to Tongcheng."

The hot, older bus travels through smaller country-side villages with many stops as Maggie dozes sitting in narrow double seat. Next year after arriving in Tongcheng for second contract October 2017, later in college term because of details of authentications of documents at Chinese Consulate in home country, plans to register second time is one-day return-trip within thirty days to Hangzhou.

Maggie is riding past on pink e-bike while walking to canteen for supper on warm afternoon day after arriving feeling very refreshed after summer vacation said, "You must travel to Hangzhou tomorrow and register at Bureau of Exits and Entrances in Hangzhou."

Replying is in shock with news and said, "Why? How? Return-trip is sixteen hours."

Next morning leave Tongcheng for Hefei fast train station early in morning with carpool of students and David visiting capitol's college in Hefei. The group will greet same-day five hour return-trip at Hefei fast train station at end of day. Days earlier after arriving on fast train from Shanghai to Hangzhou, take instructions from Eva for subway from fast train station to downtown Hangzhou to meet Echo Education assistant next morning to attend to foreigners' medical tests. Taking subway in darkness to downtown Hangzhou for check-in at same, familiar hotel from previous year after departing subway, feel lost outside subway entrance and ask for help from woman. Young man agrees to help first suggesting transit rental bicycles as hotel is nearby but decline and hire taxi as young man agrees to help with check-in from picture of hotel Justin prints-off before departure to China many hours earlier.

This morning taking fast train from Hefei to Hangzhou bring along food snacks with subway instructions from Eva, adviser to foreign teachers, to meet new intern from Echo Education in mid day and register at Hangzhou Bureau of Exits and Entrances in early afternoon in downtown Hangzhou. After texting and meeting outside subway at street level, we walk around small block to Bureau of Exits and Entrances. One woman is aggressively street begging outside Bureau angering young female intern yelling said, "You cheat. You should not be here."

Inside Bureau, on second floor wait for turn together sitting on second-floor waiting room chairs and walk to long counter to register as foreigner. Within one hour and leaving passport for registration, employer's intern assistant books return fast train ticket from Hangzhou to Hefei. On metro train to fast train station, male passenger standing glances at details of fast train ticket with surprise at time limitations and chats said, "Impressive new city developments for Hefei, and is fast growing centre."

After arriving at Hangzhou vast fast train station ask for help from young confident looking male stranger who looks at ticket departure time, and speaks English said, "We must rush," and starts to run to lead through stairways and through fast train station helping with passing security, like an emergency, in very large fast train station.

After five, four fast trains, arrive in Hefei fast train station and look for David who is to meet for car trip to Tongcheng. Student assistant, Crystal, purchases food from KFC as thoughtful gesture to eat in car trip returning to Tongcheng college late in evening. In darkness at ten pm and after Crystal helps returning to apartment in Tongcheng, Eva second Echo Education foreign adviser in Hangzhou after Lynn, is relieved to hear of safe arrival in apartment in our text messages Eva requests for confirmation of one day trip.

Negotiating to complete second contract in November 2017, is assisted by original headhunter from FindWorkAbroad hiring to come to China a year and half earlier. Able to contact Liyin on WeChat text to explain, "Require permission to return to Hangzhou to collect passport with receipt from Bureau after leaving passport thirty days earlier with Hangzhou Bureau of Exits and Entrances."

With expiring Z Visa forcing departure from second ten-month contract and China, Liyin offers advice to share with Hangzhou employer, Echo Education, replying with text said, "There is not much time."

Returning to Hangzhou for passport with passport paper receipt from Hangzhou Bureau is discussion with Maggie in apartment suggesting to mail passport receipt in dependable China Mail with request to Hangzhou Bureau to return passport in China Mail. Maggie calls David for advice who explains to Maggie passport is like Chinese ID cards people always carry.

"Do you carry your ID card?" I said.

Maggie said, "I carry ID card when leaving Tongcheng but do not carry official ID card in Tongcheng."

Arguments develop over control of passport and passport receipt. Distraught, and emotional Eva, listens to issue in cellphone.

I said, "This is chaos for foreign teachers throughout China returning to Hangzhou and long distances to travel after arriving at teaching locations to register."

Meanwhile manager Cloris of Echo Education is negotiating with Maggie in phone call. Deal is struck to return to Hangzhou to visit

Bureau of Exits and Entrances to sign for return of passport for new Foreign Resident Permit with Bureau's receipt carrying like-a-passport in replacement.

After our phone calls, Maggie, as sit together at apartment table said, "Text and ask Eva for costs of hotel to stay one night."

Eva agrees to arrange and pay hotel costs for overnight stay.

Next day repeat car trip to Hefei with David and assistant and fast train to Hangzhou. After arriving take same subway trip to downtown Hangzhou Exits and Entrances Bureau on Friday afternoon to meet Cloris, manager from Echo Education. Cloris arriving said, "Bureau closes Friday afternoons. What about supper? You are so nice."

We walk short distance to MacDonald's restaurant where huge decorated Christmas tree stands outside in mid November. Choosing small meal from lighted board, two European female foreigners stand nearby, and Cloris walks together to check-in at same hotel as in arriving in Hangzhou both years and eat restaurant meal in hotel room. Next morning, Saturday, Cloris arrives at hotel after hotel buffet breakfast and give MacDonald's children toys included in meal to Cloris for her child next morning she accepts. Cloris's husband, driving SUV, and child with them, together travel to Bureau of Exits and Entrances. Cloris buys drinks from vending machine at top of stairs before passing through security table with information checking. After checking in at long counter, walk across from long counter to smaller table twenty feet away for passport with second, new Permanent Resident Permit's, 30 November 2017, stamp into passport handed over from small file cabinet and female clerk. Cloris suggests restroom on main floor before departing. The couple drive to Hangzhou fast train station, Cloris pays and buys fast train ticket.

While falling asleep on fast train, passengers yelling said, "Missing stop!"

Getting off next stop past Hefei at Nanjing dash to buy return ticket at security office loading area for passengers for short distance to return to Hefei stop. Male security is helpful and asks for extra costs and gives instructions in English to return to fast train. On train female security attendant questions and asks to pay for new ticket.

While trying to show receipt for extra cost already paid, man nearby asks of location of foreigner's work interrupts said to female attendant said, "Leave alone."

Maggie arrives in Hefei in SUV and college driver meeting at five pm. Back in Tongcheng, Maggie arranges supper at restaurant nearby college and includes driver to share supper. Driver attempts teaching Mandarin as sits on right Saturday evening, and Maggie walks together few blocks back to college apartment.

Months into second contract, needing to transfer Permit to Anqing from Hangzhou, Maggie arrives after texting early one morning in winter holiday to visit second Bureau in Anqing, for Province of Anhui Bureau of Exits and Entrances to register for Permit in January and leave passport for second thirty days with Anqing Bureau issuing second receipt. While waiting for Bureau to review details and return enjoy quiet lunch together in very same restaurant year and half earlier. We wait again for co-op taxi in building near Bureau where taxi meets and we return to Tongcheng in darkness. Taxi driver pulls into taxi stop to gas up and wait short time for taxi to return to college. Returning with group of students and Chinese teacher in carpool to Anqing Bureau in February 2018, stop in at Bureau, go for lunch at same restaurant from first visit to Anqing to wait and retrieve passport with transfer and new registration. Payment is made from college by Maggie. Blue sticker is attached to passport from Bureau of Exits and Entrances in Anqing.

I said, "Please translate blue sticker from Bureau on passport?"

Maggie translating said, "June, date for renewal."

"Nice to return to Tongcheng. Thank you," I said.

Days later we walk to Tongcheng Bureau of Exits and Entrances to transfer permit from Anqing to Tongcheng, and for third time leave passport for paper receipt. Few days later return to Tongcheng Bureau for passport as classes in March spring term begin and Maggie pays fees. As sit across from familiar female police officer after coming to Tongcheng and staying in hotel day after arrival in September 2016, police officer said, "You are able to return and start term."

FINAL FLIGHT HOME

On 01 July 2018, flying from Shanghai Pudong international airport feels like the end of long course or trip. The flight is at least ten hours and automatically put on ear phone headset on airplane as soon as headsets are distributed by flight attendants. Trip to and from China four times in two years is familiar and distractions of movies, music or podcasts are more restful experiences to sit and listen or even fall asleep. The travellers blog reading before departing for China in 2016, suggests bringing light poncho to wear on flight for warmth and helps to decide to wear same unlined easy wear jacket departing on flight to China in 2016.

The jacket feels hot and awkward over two layers of clothes in hot day August 2016, sitting with two sons at airport over coffee and departure-send-off and Justin said, "Aren't you hot?"

I said, "Yes, but wear extra layers of clothes for long stay away."

Newer backpack is larger first-aide style scavenge from home garbage bin holding laptop computer storing in flight's overhead compartment. The black canvas bag with clothes is checked with Shanghai Pudong international airport flight company. Blankets and small pillows and choices of meal entries from flight attendants help with comfort and warmth in mid morning to arrive one hour late at noon 01 July. Excitement develops seeing coastline after nine months and grateful occasion to take photographs with both Ipad and cellphone. Departure dinner is two days earlier at TongCheng Jinrui Gujing Hotel Friday evening 27 June 2018.

Only this week Maggie said, "Head Master Wu invites us to dinner and celebrate and say goodbye on Friday night."

Information is final message from Tongcheng to son, Mark, from TongCheng sent 26 June 2018. Mark quickly replies to text from South Korea asking name of restaurant, and make note of difficult name from sign at restaurant to share.

At our final dinner, Headmaster Wu with some English translations from Maggie said, "Aware of plan for shipping of suitcase before departing and offer my compliments," glancing to left as sits beside on right at farewell celebration dinner.

Maggie is sitting on left.

"Senior sophomore student, Joy, assists with translations for English instructions to clerks at the college's shipping office where Joy is also a customer at same time. Joy said, 'Helping is opportunity Chinese teacher advises to practice English translations for output.'"

"Four thousand yuan is amount," I said.

Maggie said, "Costs of shipping seem high."

Seating at official dinner is similar to our Winter break end-of-term celebrations with President Shen sitting to Head Master's immediate right, next to Dean of Physics, and Dean of English, who is English as Foreign Language teacher primary supervisor. To left is Maggie and beside Maggie's left are two student assistants, Crystal and Stephanie. Beautifully decorated round table with exceptional exotic food is carved into shapes in variety of animals. Sculptured deer from pumpkin and radish sits on a plate with fried rolled tofu. Headmaster Wu enjoys pointing out food shapes of animals and together decide on English words for animal illustrations in food.

David sits across table giving thumbs-up to vague work plans after departure of online teaching English as Foreign Language speaks-up in English said, "Foreigners expect," and Head Master raises his hand to quiet Dean of English.

Head Master Wu and President Shen speak Chinese to each other continuously throughout meal and with Dean of Physics. At conclusion of dinner, President Shen takes many photos with Headmaster and group photo and Maggie prints next day and frames but must remove photos from frames for suitcase and leave frames for neighbours. After arriving at Tongcheng College, if encountering crossing street to college gate or on college campus, Headmaster Wu always smiles with friendly wave or stops to chat, and arranges year earlier in first ten-month contract to meet Head Master's wife, Hong Wei, in January 2017, with college's invitation.

In next couple days 30 June 2018, and late afternoon arrival at Shanghai Honquoi fast train station from Hefei, carry black canvas bag and wear heavy back pack through long concourse for taxi to drive one hour to Pudong international airport. Avoiding airport directions in signs to Honquoi international airport, walk down long concourse filled with restaurants meeting man with sign offering taxi.

Younger man begins to ask of flight departure plans speaking English, and offers taxi rate agreeable to drive to Pudong international airport but said, "What about time of departure from Shanghai?"

So confessing said, "Plan is to sleep at airport. Departure time is following morning."

Taxi salesman said, "Sleeping at airport is not good," shaking his head. "Suggest choice of hotels with five star and very high rate or hotel like hostel so cost much less."

Elating relief and pleasure said, "Choose less expensive for rest and sleep before departure next morning."

Departing concourse follow downstairs to parking lot and waiting black unmarked taxi resembling limousine service in Beijing in July 2017. Now driver and salesman with discussions evolving make phone call about hotel said, "Choose hostel-price with airport shuttle."

Taxi salesman smiles and driver makes arrangements for hostel-like-hotel and leaves. In car for one-hour trip to hotel near Shanghai Pudong International Airport, water bottles sit nearby on backseat in black luxury-like sedan with leather seats and said to driver, "*Li*?"

Driver is agreeing with nodding.

The street and arrival area is filled with lighted signs in darkness of early evening and driver looks for small hotel and seeing lighted-sign driver motions to small hotel. The streets are thick rows of brightly-lit, abundant, colourful street signs and in imagination from reading about vibrant Shanghai decades ago and feel adventure is continuing in Shanghai. The driver parks and collects black canvas bag from limousine's trunk and wearing backpack enter small hotel together. Limousine driver explains introductions at smaller lobby desk in front to left with one female hotel clerk managing and male clerk nearby both checking information.

Showing passport and Z Visa to female hotel clerk, female hotel clerk looks closely at passport and Z Visa as she questions and points said, "Explain type of Visa."

I said to clerk, "Z Visa is because of employment as English as Foreign Language teacher from Anhui," and clerk returns passport. While paying clerks for one night stay, ask about the airport shuttle too.

The male clerk said, "Come to desk in morning and wait on bench opposite lobby desk at eight am," and limousine driver leaves.

The female clerk passes room-key with floor and room number, and with her hand and head motions to walk to elevator at end of lobby of small hotel. Elevator and hallways are clean and quiet and find floor to small hotel's room. Private room is surprising with double bed, a modern bathroom and working TV. With good movie in English showing, eat food in room packing from Tongcheng, take shower, rest in bed to watch movie and text Hong and Maggie.

"Staying overnight in Shanghai in small hotel before depart in morning."

Maggie texting back said, "Ok."

Hong texting said, "Hello Maria. Have you arrived at the hotel successfully? Have you had dinner? Goody. Are you ok? May you always be happy. This is your last night in China maybe. May you have a good dream."

Packing up next morning black bag seems smaller unable to close zipper and leave behind more small things. Checking-out at hotel's front desk, leave room key and wait quietly alone. Deciding to walk out of hotel to shuttle bus waiting in front with backpack and carrying black canvas bag to bus driver with gestures said, "Pudong?"

Driver is nodding permission and offering to store black canvas bag in storage area of shuttle bus. Finding seat midway near front and wearing backpack, feel warmth in morning's busy streets of clear blue skies in Shanghai. Shuttle bus fills with passengers, and two young female foreigners waiting on street board shuttle bus. Driver is speaking to another Chinese passenger for most of one hour to Pudong International Airport through quiet streets and few morning walkers, workers or shoppers in sunshine, grassy parks and magical wide blue sky Saturday morning. At Pudong arrivals within hour, driver jumps out and retrieves luggage for passengers, and offers assistance retrieving luggage cart from entrance area for black canvas bag and backpack parting.

Returning to international airport is same day on sunny Saturday 01 July, as leaving Shanghai, China on 01 July, as Asia is more than twelve hours ahead in timeline. Two sons drive to international airport to meet, and hoping to look very well for greeting, clothes are charcoal dress slacks, a new light blue shirt never worn before and slip on black shoes without laces to come untied worn for departing to China in August 2016. The long walk down entrance to international airport from air flight company's arrival ramp is familiar from previous year. In arrival area, all citizens are directed in one direction and fewer foreigners another to complete self check-ins with passports. The lengthy citizen lineup to check-in with passport is majority of returning Chinese expatriates. Passport self-check-ins are in multiple rows of machines smaller than size of gasoline pumps. The self check-in machine refuses to accept passport. Moving outside self check-in passport location, two or three clerks request passengers fill in Declaration forms at small desk and view passports for check-in before going to line-up to border agents in rows of glass cubicle offices further past desk. The male border clerk looks in curious way asking to wait as he looks for passport self check-in clerk behind roped off area of self-check-in machines few feet away. Female clerk asks to point out location of self check-in machine failing to accept passport which is nearby Declaration desk, accepts explanation after pointing out self check-in machine and male passport clerk motions to next line-up to Border Agents.

Lines to go through Border Security are in next nearby location in airport's arrival area. Joining twisting line-up like a stomach's intestine move towards Border Agents sitting nearby at glassed windows of raised desks enclosing booth-like offices with speaking openings and in one row. |One suitcase is left in our intestine line everyone begins staring at and passengers begin discussions wondering whose suitcase is left and one male in front yells to border security guard said, "Suitcase is left."

Nearby our group is one security guard and steps in to put suitcase aside. The line-up is within half an hour to reach Border Security in glassed-in booths in one row to speak through window to border agent. The female border agent's abrupt, brisk questions inquire of departure date to China and views passport.

I said, "Last October 2017, with contract as English as foreign language teacher in Anhui, China."

The female border agent says nothing and stamps passport to continue Entry into country. The previous year after being abroad for eleven months in August 2017, male border agent sits at much smaller open podium-desk near passport check-in and looks at photo taken at automatic passport check-in, compares to passport photo and views to decide to allow entry and taking only few minutes.

Returning to Shanghai, China in October 2017, after longer-than-plan summer vacation seems simpler when Chinese airport guard stands nearby directing smaller lineup of few older foreigner tourists, and few much younger females chatting about later meeting. Standing in floor's painted footprints on tiled floor to wait turns, female border agent sitting in eye level island desk speaks behind glass, looks at new and second Z Visa, and waives through smiling said, "Welcome back to China."

Walking past police officers and security guards outside border security, lighted signboards with directions describe flight arrivals directing passengers to walk to correct moving luggage arrivals in long rectangular. Finding luggage carts nearby walk around luggage arrival carousel and to far end with luggage cart away from crowd of passengers to wait as male Border Guard brings official search dog to start climbing over all luggage on the arrival's moving slanted deck carousel. The dog is friendly-looking, large, taffy-colour, full breed. Black canvas bag comes toward to grab and put on luggage cart with heavy backpack. The long line-up at Border Entrance for arrivals into airport after retrieving luggage is longest wait and longest line with Border guard near front of lineup.

Younger-looking woman gets out of line-up as she gets closer to the border guard checking arrival and declaration cards and he said, "Where are you going?"

Passengers ignore the border guard and younger woman walks away, and the line moves along. Border guard glances at Declaration Card without comment to allow to continue on to arrival area and through Entrance to international airport. Justin meets alone previous year at same airport returning after first year in China in August 2017, after ten months in Tongcheng, and one month training in Beijing. Entering country from entrance with group of passengers in roped-off area of airport Justin said, "Mom."

Turning to look behind see in relief tall blonde young man, Justin, standing and walk towards the rope as security guard behind son smiles and lifts rope to hug son welcoming flight from Beijing and suggests Tim Horton's coffee in airport arrivals.

First glimpses are Patrick, second oldest son, in distance waving and see Justin, youngest son, beside Patrick all waving. Both sons are smiling, lineup progresses smoothly, and hug them. Patrick picks up black canvas bag and quickly leave international airport at exit to park-aide to find white sedan, left with Justin while working past two years in China. After Justin pays for parking at machine outside park-aide, Justin drives and Patrick sits in back seat driving out of international airport park-aide. Justin suggests sharing lunch as driving along freeway. Asking about their supportive paternal grandmother, Helen, is in thoughts before departing TongCheng for first conversation with sons after arrival returning 01 July 2018. Patrick explains grandmother is in hospital for hip issues. Helen describes getting university degrees important, married or not. Months later during summer vacations Patrick helps in visit 22 July 2019, after returning home.

In her 100th year Helen said, "I feel the same as in younger times. It's over before you know it."

In warm, sunny Vancouver afternoon sit side-by-side as Helen enjoys one cigarette in area manager arranges outdoors for Helen sitting on lawn chairs in circle on wide private lawns with Patrick and Helen's daughter enjoying our chance to visit again. We begin chatting by cellphone months earlier and continue after visiting.

Driving down freeway discussion erupts to suggest popular fast food restaurants. Everyone agrees to MacDonald's sign in view for lunch. Justin parks white sedan and together walk inside to order lunch from automatic order machine near front door and mention machine is in same restaurant franchise in Hangzhou sharing story of ordering meal with Cloris, employment adviser from similar machine with pictures describing meal suggestions. Lunch order arrives and each pay and Patrick buys lunch for two and ask for cup of coffee with Justin buying his own. Coffee, soft drinks and burgers arrive to sit quietly together on outdoor patio enjoying restaurant food and mention great cup of coffee.

Patrick's first conversation laughing said, "Who put family's BBQ together? Someone from work?"

"I guess so," I said. "Trip from TongCheng to Shanghai on fast train goes well. Thanks for waiting after flight's one hour delay in Shanghai. Passengers sit in boarding location around gate on floor or in chairs waiting for departure."

Both sons begin laughing said, "We worry about being late ourselves learning of delay from airport website to enjoy cup of coffee together."

"Grateful to both for all efforts to meet arriving from China. Hong Wei, friend and wife of college's Head Master, asks if we can take arriving selfie photograph to share on WeChat with new friend, Hong Wei? During our first meeting in Anqing Hong tells Anqing is rich with culture and boasts new chemical plant creating wealth and of her only son, an engineering student abroad in Germany."

We do group hug with arms around each for selfie on sunny restaurant patio. A few people are sitting at tables on quiet patio restaurant. Patrick leaving for ferry terminal to travel home to new location since departing to China two years before, walks away waving and smiling down the street towards metro train.

Justin offering invitation for departure home, agree and walk towards white sedan in the fast food parking lot and drive one hour to Justin's home, and ask to stay few days to rest as fatigue feels too great to drive many hours. While working in Toncheng Justin marrying girlfriend, and after arrival at their home enjoy piece of wedding cake, a request to bride to save for sharing. Justin and bride sit nearby on red couch. "Special peach-like filling is in between layers," bride and groom said, "is for Blush And Blue theme of wedding."

Larger travel suitcase, Justin's bride donates and packs to travel to China in 2016, arrives from Shanghai sent by the Tongcheng College shipping company and sits in front entrance. Justin missing being home for delivery picks up suitcase from delivery office. Departing Hefei, and carrying heavy suitcase up vast fast train departure staircase is too arduous. The large, thick, metal, aluminum clothing rack sits wrapped in shipping bags next to large black suitcase and delivery from Shanghai is separate, arriving by FedEx with Justin home for delivery. Little welsh terrier white dog, Wesley, is very special to take on long walks together while visiting for weeks before returning to Tongcheng waiting for Z Visa approval many months earlier. In next days complete oil change in car and depart for mountainous drive to permanent home.

Relaxing and unpacking belongings find four drawings, eleven times fourteen inches, on thick paper with pastel crayon images of dancing hand-holding children, country scenes with hearts, homes and flowers. Gift package of two large tea tins resembling tea on shelf at Tongcheng supermarket is shipped ahead in larger suitcase. Before departing

Tongcheng in June 2017, the same shipping office at Tongcheng College make arrangements to ship six large tins of tea to Patrick. Shipping tea gift in cargo costs a-lot-more from airline's check-in Patrick seeing many times from travel, and airlines inflicting travellers with high shipping costs believing gifts as carry-on with bags for flights.

Laying children's drawings around living room and dining area, enjoy pictures of original drawings from Chinese children given at Tongcheng's training school in January 2018. David, Dean of English translates into Chinese as speak English to room full with training school younger children and parents in presentation at invitation of training school. David's wife is managing training school for owner David's sister and husband. David promising in car leaving restaurant to return children's drawings and arranging to locate gift of drawings from children left in small plastic red shopping bag at restaurant attending for supper afterwards. Weeks later, after returning to apartments in same building following faculty's invitation to celebration at restaurant meal, get locked-out of second-floor apartment's automatic door lock and leaving apartment key inside. After returning from meal and texting David, a neighbour in apartment building, we wait for apartment building manager in David's apartment on sixth-floor 24 March 2018. During visit waiting for apartment building manager, David returns children's gift of colourful drawings in red plastic bag he collects forgotten in restaurant after attending training school in January. Sharing news of youngest son's wedding this day visiting and waiting, David lowers his chin.

"Youngest son shares all wedding planning details. We are able to text each other minutes before wedding ceremony begins. Youngest son clarifies will feel too bad if left contract and China for wedding," I said.

Plastic bottles full of wax crayons, bringing to China in August 2016, drawing and colouring in leisure time and filling with water for weights to carry twice a week at college's playground, unpack too. When returning to college previous October 2017, settling into new apartment location on college campus, Maggie picks up bottles sitting on shelf in bedroom staring at colourful crayons inside.

Explaining in few words said, "Bringing for leisure time."

Much later in a telephone call, Mark said. "Experiences of quietness is after foreign and overseas experience with large populations and large cities and contrasts with less populated and smaller cities."

Everything seems small. Inquiring about returning to Tongcheng with Hangzhou employer evolve with Maggie and family are supportive.

"Not good," on WeChat Maggie writes and said, "You are missed by students and colleagues."

Eva, former foreign teacher adviser for employer from Hangzhou said, "College is no longer their client and employer can no longer apply for Z Visa due to new age restrictions."

Patrick asking about decision to leave working as English as Foreign Language teacher in Tongcheng said, "Is there difficulty from hiring professional travel agency to apply for Z Visa instead of Chinese Visa Centre as apply to in 2016?"

Trying to agree said, "planning by College signing an employment contract in September is after work permit application from Hangzhou employer and Hangzhou Bureau approval. Travel for permanent residency is between two provinces to three Chinese Bureaus of Exits and Entrances government offices forcing many lengthy trips. College did not want to renew Z visa."

TongCheng College Contract 2nd year, China, AnHui,

Poetry November 29, 2017

"My things have arrived from storage"

D e l i c i o u s

My Red Filter

The plastic is darkened

I had missed my gift

The instant style gained a laugh

So I enjoy my first brew.

Storage had not gone well

One item is lost

So I get help

And I may get compensation!

The clothes rack is special to me

Luxury I think

They break easily

But this one was better.

I think I can stay

But paper problems create

Opportunities I did not see

I wait, hey passport.

So I say I am grateful. 16:00 November 29, 2017 Wednesday Maulo

Designer's Photograph

A lure of the image

Makes us proud

To others

Who enjoys the effect

Of the moment to capture

We do not know

Practice and style attract

I know I am impressed

Who lives in the effect

No one pays, no one stays

Off they are but where

A photographer may leave.

Maulo

November 30, 2017 09:51

Daily walking five to ten kilometres and writing in journal in daily walk schedule is described much earlier in free verse from 2012, #filthydirtybuttonart free verse poetry.

HARSH APERTURES September 22, 2012

Shooting the roll

Even one day to advance "24"

Harsh apertures in our soul

"In a few seconds?" to be more.

"Swords" "I had to fill in the lines"

Four lines of words

Unfinished shines

To buff the thought "swords". Maulo

Index of Twenty Samples for Conversations from Topics in *Essences of Tongcheng*

1. Activities,
    - Hiking
    - Shopping
    - Walking

2. Animals,
    - Dogs
    - Mouse
    - Salamander
    - Squirrel

3. Apartments,
    - Apartment building 2017-2018
    - Dormitory building 2016-2017

4. Banks,
    - Bank of China
    - China Merchants Bank

5. Cities in China,
    - Anqing
    - Beijing
    - Hangzhou
    - Hefei

Nanjiing
Shanghai
Tongcheng

6. College buildings and locations,
    Academic buildings
    Boulevard
    Canteen
    Dormitories
    English as Foreign language classrooms
    Gate
    Gatehouse
    Lecture theatre building
    Playground
    Shipping offices

7. College Staff
    Maggie
    Shen, President
    Sue
    Wang, David
    Wu, Hong Wei
    Wu, Headmaster
    Ye, Mr.

8. Drinks,
    Beer
    Coffee
    Corn shake
    Green tea

9. Festivals in China,
    Dragon Boat
    Moon
    New Year's
    Spring
    Tomb-Sweeping

10. Fast Train

11. Food,
    - Apples
    - Bananas
    - Chicken
    - Congee
    - Eggs
    - Fish
    - Mango
    - Noodles
    - Persimmons
    - Rice
    - Spareribs
    - Tofu

12. Hostel

13. Hotels

14. Metro Trains,
    - Beijing
    - Hangzhou

15. Photographs,
    - Tongcheng Teachers College
    - New building site for Tongcheng Teachers College
    - Student-led English Corner
    - Hiking with Maggie
    - Farewell Dinner
    - Guniubei Reservoir
    - Long Mian River
    - Jingzhu Temple

16. Stores and Restaurants,

    7-11
    KFC
    MacDonalds
    Supermarket

17. Students,

    Amy
    Annie
    Crystal
    Donna
    Elinor
    Joanna
    Joy
    Joyce
    Stephanie
    Tiffany

18. Suitcase,

    Bedding
    Clothes
    Hats
    Shoes

19. Temples,

    Anqing Buddhist Temple
    Confucian Temple National historic site Tongcheng City Square
    Tongcheng Mountain local temple

20. Tutoring English as Foreign Language

Dear Readers

Nowadays Maggie, students at Tongcheng Teachers College and former students, some pursuing teaching, family life or other career choices continue relationship-building by sharing stories with our social media English Corner and in our private chats.

To ask after them or with your own inquiry do let me know by writing via email at:

mhjarmstrong@icloud.com

Printed in the United States
by Baker & Taylor Publisher Services